AUGUSTINE AND SPINOZA

Augustine
AND
Spinoza

Milad Doueihi

Translated by Jane Marie Todd

HARVARD UNIVERSITY PRESS
Cambridge, Massachusetts
London, England
2010

Copyright © 2010 by the President and Fellows of Harvard College
All rights reserved
Printed in the United States of America

Publication of this book has been aided by a grant
from the French Ministry of Culture.
Ouvrage publié avec le concours du Ministère
français chargé de la Culture—Centre national du livre.

First published as *Solitude de l'Incomparable. Augustin et Spinoza*,
© Éditions du Seuil, 2009. Collection La Librairie du XXIe siècle
dirigée par Maurice Olender.

Library of Congress Cataloging-in-Publication Data
Doueihi, Milad.
[Solitude de l'incomparable. English]
Augustine and Spinoza / by Milad Doueihi ;
translated by Jane Marie Todd.
p. cm.
Includes bibliographical references (p. 107) and index.
ISBN 978-0-674-05063-1 (alk. paper)
1. Spinoza, Benedictus de, 1632–1677. 2. Augustine, Saint,
Bishop of Hippo. 3. Jews—Election, Doctrine of.
4. Grace (Theology) I. Title.
B3999.J8.D68 2010
220.6092'2—dc22   2010002439

Contents

Preface   vii

Introduction   1

1 Augustine, Religion as Rereading   9

2 Hobbes, or Nature as Reason   52

3 Spinoza and the "Relics of Man's Ancient Bondage"   58

Conclusion: "The Infinite Separation"   85

Notes   95
Selected Bibliography   107
Index   113

Preface

Grace and election: that pair of terms points to the complex relationship between Christianity and Judaism. Judaism is forever marked by election because it has the covenant and the Law, a pact and mutual pledge between the Creator and his people. Christianity, the "new covenant" in Augustine's philosophy, inaugurates the order of grace. At a fundamental level, grace raises the problem of faith and does so in explicit opposition to the Law. For Augustine, grace subordinates Hebrew specificity—that is, election, the covenant, and the Law—to the advent of Christianity. Without faith, the Law is blind; without Christ, election is imperfect, incomplete, condemned to error and errancy.

From the Augustinian point of view, grace constitutes the perfect mediation: between the Law and faith, the old and the new, the local and the universal, the letter and the spirit, the covenant and the church. Not surprisingly, that mediation is a *conversion* in the broad sense of the term, that is, both a return to oneself or to the starting point, and a change and transformation. Grace as mediation institutes a new order, that in which the human being is faced with a choice between, on one hand, his desires and free will, and, on the other, the selflessness of faith and the expectation of God's gift. It is in this sense that grace gives rise to what Augustine calls a "free choice," namely, one that recognizes that "faith obtains what the law commands."[1] Augustine places the commandments and the gift in opposition, to distinguish between the Law and faith: "God, therefore, commands continence; and he gives continence. He commands through the law; he gives through grace; he commands through the letter; he gives through the Spirit. For without grace the law makes sin abound, and without the spirit the letter kills."[2]

For Augustine, the Law requires the use of reason: "Since there is also a law in the reason of a human being who already uses free choice, a law naturally written in his heart, by which he is warned that he should not do anything to anyone else that he himself does not want to suffer, all are transgressors according to this law, even those who have not received the law given through Moses."[3] That utterly Judaic rationality excludes faith. Hence the key issue for Augustine, as for so many others after him, is the gap introduced by the distinction between grace and election. Benedictus de Spinoza, unlike Augustine and other Christian theologians and philosophers, resituates the Law and faith within an interpretation of human understanding and human nature. Along the way, he will opt for a different rationality that does not recognize Augustinian grace and its legacies or Augustine's insistence on the inadequacy of Hebrew election. On the contrary, Spinoza naturalizes biblical election. Election, local and national, sets a people apart, but grace is universal. That universality introduces a transmission (or rather a contagion) that passes from the first man to humankind as a whole. It is egalitarian in the realm of error and in sin, thereby authorizing the Christian fulfillment of the Law. If sin is an integral part of human nature, grace remains an act of grace, a favor, a gift to be hoped for and awaited, another election. Grace converts election even while displacing it: "When God says, 'Turn ye unto me, and I will turn unto you,' [*Convertimini ad me, et convertar ad vos*], one of these clauses—that which invites our return [*convertamur*] to God—evidently belongs to our will; while the other, which promises His return to us [*convertatur*], belongs to His grace."[4] Grace is the agency of conversion, of any conversion, that of the covenant and the Law as well as that of election and reason.

How are we to explain, beyond the historical relationship between Judaism and Christianity, the survival and philosophical legacy of the grace/election pair? What are the connections between that legacy and the gap between reason and faith, between the will and the freedom to philosophize, and between authority and rationality? These are some of the questions elicited by a comparison between Augustine's and Spinoza's thinking on the subject of biblical election.

Some chapters of this book were the subject of a course I taught at the Scuola di Alti Studi, Fondazione San Carlo, in Modena, Italy, in May 2008. My thanks to Michelina Borsari for her invitation and to the students who urged me to expand on my readings. Other themes were developed in Maurice Olender's seminar at the École des Hautes Études en Sciences Sociales.

AUGUSTINE AND SPINOZA

Introduction

My aim in this book is elementary: to examine, through the texts of Augustine and Spinoza, the articulation of a problem, that of election. How are we to account for election within a theological and philosophical framework, and what are the methodological and epistemological processes that explain Augustine's and Spinoza's major analyses? Furthermore, how are we to account for the similarities, surprising as they may be, between their two approaches, without forgetting or neglecting the radical differences in their objectives and methods? The question of election, in calling for an explanation of the nature and consequences of what makes a covenant possible and of what sets in motion a founding contract between a creator God and his chosen people, leads almost naturally (and, for Spinoza and Augustine, even necessarily) to an inquiry into history. It also prompts an inquiry into the nature of historical discourse, its motives, and especially its truth. The models for the construction, transmission, and reception of historical discourse constitute unique sites for studying the privileged relationship between a people and its history as the unparalleled vehicle of its intimate relationship with its God.

Election, it is true, does not allow for comparison. It would seem to be a solitary traveler. At the most simple level, it is an identity, the mark of a distinction, the sign of a choice, but also and especially of a destiny forged by the consequences of a unique and primordial separation. Election is also a privilege and a surplus that, in history, name and found the specificity of a collectivity. But election is above all a bearing witness, an act of exchange, and an economy between the elect and the elector, the chosen and the chooser. Nevertheless, in efforts to represent and recuperate election, appeals have continually been made to what election is not or cannot be. Both Augustine and Spinoza—each in his own way—do no more than configure that election to fit their own systems: that of grace in one case, that of the freedom to philosophize in the other. We need only follow and retrace the paths of their spiritual or intellectual systems.

Clearly, the Doctor of Grace and the author of the *Theological-Political Treatise* are not generally likened to each other. The connection made between Augustine and Spinoza may be considered surprising. How are we to justify this pairing, this comparison, which at first sight appears rash, even arbitrary? It seems to me that we have only to examine certain problems that preoccupied both authors. It will then become evident that the Doctor of Grace and the author of the *Theological-Political Treatise* have in common a large number of questions that they raised and studied over the course of their writing lives. How, then, are we to explain these affinities, which seem so fortuitous and so disconcerting?

The question of election, like that of grace, posits the Bible as the *site* of *method*, of any *method*; and method is a practice of reading. That practice requires a reflection on the nature of reading in general and on its effects on the apprehension—as well as the transmission and reception—of truths or, in some cases, of errors and superstitions. Between Spinoza and Augustine, between election and grace, everything is played out in the *ways of reading* and the *manners of saying*. Election is thus constitutive of a specific reading, which orchestrates not only the philological and textual analysis but also the theological and political dimensions of the philology. And that philology in some sense forms a society and governs a *city*. Reading is also, in the first place, a *political act*, a determining choice that governs and informs the organization of the social, of its fundamental categories, while legitimating the identity-based distinctions within the city. Thus it is not surprising that meditations on what reading means occupy a central place in Augustine's and Spinoza's writings. Quite simply, how are we to read texts in the first place? How are we to interpret manifestations of grace or of signs of the covenant? How are we to read the biblical texts recounting the exchanges between God and human beings, and what kinship do these ways of reading have with both religion and philosophy? What is the status of the Law, its origin, its genesis, its historicity, and above all, its finality?

It is the problem of election, with everything it implies within theology and philosophy, that offers us the best entry into that unexplored territory between Spinoza and Augustine. By the term "election" we must first understand the status and specificity of the Old Testament and the status of the Jewish people as it is constructed by the covenant. But we must also consider within this context the theoretical or theological developments that negotiate and attempt to make intelligible and acceptable the transition from the Old Testament to the New, or, as is too often repeated, from the particular to the universal. Election sets in place a whole series of key concepts that both Augustine and Spinoza will analyze: symbol; covenant and contract; prophecy and revelation; miracle and superstition; mediation and vision; the nature of collective identity and of its political models; genealogy and conversion.

In both authors, then, we find a critical examination of Old Testament prophecy and an assessment of the veracity and nature of the manifestations of the divine in the Old Testament. At first glance, and despite their radical differences, Augustine and Spinoza both seem to privilege the New Testament, in accordance with a problematic that identifies religious authenticity with universality. From within that problematic, there is great progress, a radical change, between the Old and the New Testament, and the difference between the two will be explained by the nature of that evolution and that change. It goes without saying that the status of Christ and of what, for lack of a better term, would have to be called "the inscription in the heart" serves completely different aims in Augustine's writings than it does in Spinoza's. Although the shift from the Old to the New Testament is marked by the emergence of a primacy given to a certain form of interiority, the nature of that "new" reality, in the view of the two authors, reflects fundamentally opposing conceptions. For Augustine, it is grace, with the openness it presupposes, that seems to be the generative principle and the regulator of human nature after the Fall. For Spinoza, human nature, through the intermediary of philosophy, aspires to an autonomy that knows nothing of grace or the hope for an intervention by the divine. But in both cases, between two poles—on one hand, nature and its connections to God and his revelation; on the other, the vicissitudes of grace and its snares—perspectives take shape that are ethical in the first instance, despite their theological import. In that sense, the reading that propels each interpretation is an argument for a way of being: for Spinoza, the human being's freedom to philosophize and his autonomy to exercise his political choices; for Augustine, the will to accept and await the divine gift of grace, with all that choice implies for the order of the city.[1]

Augustine and Spinoza both grapple with superstition.[2] Augustine's critique has two targets: first, pagan cults and gods, with the individual and collective imagination or "superstition" they entail; and second, Jewish superstition, rooted in the Law and the letter of the Law, and the confusion between the specificity of the local or regional and the absolute and universal. In the *City of God* and elsewhere,

Augustine continually rails against that literalism, which according to him blinds the chosen people and impedes authentic revelation, the truth of the Incarnation, and the proper interpretation of scripture. For him, the truth of the Incarnation requires not only a rereading of Old Testament prophecies, but also a questioning of the very possibility of a revelation, or, more precisely, of a direct manifestation of the divine under the order of the Law. In great part, that radical choice shapes Augustine's methodology. Spinoza, by contrast, sees superstition as one of the "main prejudices" of religion, that is, as one of the relics of ancient bondage, translated into blind and blinding obedience to authority. For him, literalism constitutes the first phase of the proper method for accurately reading scriptures. And, to simplify, allegory only accentuates and embellishes the distortions of theologians and substantiates received ideas about true religion. Spinoza too will attack the prophecy at the heart of the Old Testament, but in order to demonstrate the geographical and political specificity of that book, contrasting it to the universality of the truth of religion, of *his religion*.

For both authors, superstition raises fundamental questions about the legacy and historical reception of truth, and about the constitution of a tradition founded on transmission, with all the problems that follow from it. Furthermore, superstition preserves the effects of inherited misreadings in beliefs, popular practices, political reality, and ultimately in the institutions themselves. The centrality in Augustine's and Spinoza's writings of the analysis of superstition can be explained in part by the access it allows to the social dimension (in the broad sense) of the religious.

This brief summary has cast into relief the main lines of a conjunction, a revealing intersection between Augustine and Spinoza, at the site of a few big questions: the status of divine manifestation and revelation in the Old Testament; the ways of reading and interpreting the founding narratives of scripture; the similarities, and especially, the differences between the Old and New Testaments.

For these two authors, the radical and wholly determining difference is located between the Jewish "nationalism" of the Old Testament and the universalism of the New. The status of election gives rise to two models or organizing schemata of the social: the city of God and the city of the philosopher.

In Augustine's texts, grace comes into being as a function of two problems, two contexts. The first of these is the problematic and contested link between the Old and New Testaments. In Augustine's early writings, this concern reflects his struggle with the Manichaean legacy. The second problem, by contrast, arises as a direct response to the Pelagian crisis. But in the wake of his two major themes, grace and the problem of evil, Augustine softens and reworks a fundamental, even radical question: What is the status of revelations of the divine in the Old Testament? Or, more exactly, were there direct and authentic manifestations of God under the Law? That question continues to haunt and obsess Augustine; it can be found nearly everywhere in the Doctor of Grace's vast body of writings. Indeed, despite a few variations it will undergo under rhetorical or polemical constraints, that question defines and determines the principle—which is almost absolute—guiding the Augustinian interpretation of the Old Testament as a figure, and especially, as a powerful model for articulating the principles for reading the key texts of the tradition. In other words, Augustine formulates his analyses and the methodological positions he takes (regarding the image, voice, and language) as a function of a necessity: the narrative fulfillment of the Old Testament in the New. Augustine conceives of the relation between the figure and the letter in terms that, in effect, come to posit grace as a negation of an essential impossibility inscribed in the form and structure of the Law. Whereas the Law names and designates a covenant and a contract, grace refers to the absolute gift, one that incurs no debt and requires no reciprocity, and that, above all, has no need for an external, visible manifestation. The Law traces a borderline; it marks a separation, or, as Augustine will say, an exclusion. Grace, by contrast, is a universal promise that has neither limits nor boundaries. But how to legitimate that grace? To offer a few inklings of a response to that question, we need to return to some Augustinian arguments, integrating them into his recuperation of election through its best-known biblical representations.

Beyond the correspondences between Augustine and Spinoza, it is important to emphasize a more important and more revealing convergence, one that seemingly yields the secret that haunts both philosophies. By that I mean the necessity, or, if you will, the inevitability, of formulating what it is fitting to call a *symbol* (in the ancient sense of "creed"), symbol of the father of the church and symbol of the philosopher. It is then incumbent on us to observe how completely different purposes can lurk within two approaches that could not be more similar. It is that unexpected proximity that may account for the full pertinence of the comparison. In a sense, what follows is a consideration of *reading* as a constitutive act of the religious in Augustine's and Spinoza's texts. On one hand, Christianity is dedicated to rereading and (certainly for Augustine) to rereading the self—as well as what precedes it—in the signs of its future. On the other, Judaism is a reading of the present, of what *is*, of what constitutes its unique identity and distinguishes it from all the rest: reading as choice and self-affirmation, as absolute gesture of autonomy, of freedom, and of autonomization.

That cleavage between reading and reading, between reading and rereading, grace and election, also traces the contours and limits of possible comparisons, or, in other words, of the incomparable.

Christianity is incomparable because, at least for Augustine, it establishes a comparison through a gesture of absolute closure. It conceives of itself as the culmination and finality of a tradition, its ultimate fulfillment and perfection. It compares in order to absorb, to better identify what belongs to it and, in a sense, what has always belonged to it, what returns to it in accordance with its own logic. Christianity does so in order to grant itself its true identity and to render its authenticity, veiled under the supposed error of literal misreading. It must necessarily compare to put an end to comparison, to any comparison, to define itself as and through its figures and its readings.

Judaism, by contrast, is incomparable because it takes the form of a detachment, a separation or setting apart, a *distinction*, even while erecting itself as the guardian of history, of its own history in the first place, then quite simply of the history of election, and even of historicity period. If it does not regard the other, it regards itself, in its interiority, in order to compare itself in anticipation.

This book, then, is in Friedrich Nietzsche's sense both philological and untimely: "I must say so in virtue of my profession as a classical philologist, for I do not know what meaning classical philology may have for our time except in its being 'untimely'—that is, contrary to our time, and yet with an influence on it for the benefit, it may be hoped, of a future time."[3]

1

Augustine, Religion as Rereading

> It is true, therefore, that many are called but few chosen. Those are chosen who are effectually [*congruenter*] called.
>
> Augustine, "To Simplician—Questions on Various Subjects" 1.2.13, p. 395

Augustine is a pedagogue because scripture is obscure. That obscurity necessitates a learning process and the development of a methodology capable of setting aside misreadings, of overcoming the difficulties attributable to not knowing Hebrew and Greek. Reading and learning to read are essential activities because they have to do with the divine message, its articulation, its diverse manifestations, and its reception. Augustine's starting point on that pedagogical path could not be more simple: the materiality of expression, both oral and written. That founding of a Christian method or—to borrow the title of Augustine's book—of a Christian doctrine, sets in place a series of questions and problems that are at the heart of the Augustinian conception of grace, the Law, and election, and of the connections between reading and Christianity. The history of humankind in its relation with the divine can be summed up as the history of successive readings of the divine message. That history focuses on the complex play between signs and meanings, between spoken words, letters, and the will of God:

But because vibrations in the air soon pass away and remain no longer than they sound, signs of words have been constructed by means of letters. Thus words are shown to the eyes, not in themselves but through certain signs which stand for them. These signs could not be common to all peoples because of the sin of human dissension [*dissensionis humanae*] which arises when one people seizes the leadership for itself. A sign of this pride [*superbia signum*] is that tower erected [to] the heavens where impious men deserved that not only their minds but also their voices should be dissonant.

Thus it happened that even the Sacred Scripture, by which so many maladies of the human will are cured, was set forth in one language [*una lingua projecta*], but so that it could be spread conveniently through all the world it was scattered far and wide in the various languages of translators that it might be known for the salvation of peoples who desired to find in it nothing more than the thoughts and desires of those who wrote it and through these the will of God, according to which we believe those writers spoke.[1]

The diversity of languages is here placed within a narrative that translates biblical history into a history of meaning, casting into relief an evolution and a necessity. The evolution consists of an alienation from the first language; the necessity lies within the very nature of the word. But that historical semiotics has its history in the Augustinian corpus as well, from Augustine's early writings to his last texts; and that history remains relatively constant, with only a few minor variations. Beyond the impressive survival of that problematic, it is incumbent on us to ponder its constitutive elements and their relationship to the elaboration and legitimation of an economy of grace. We also need to examine what Augustine says about the text of the Old Testament, its materiality, its reception, and its transmission, its controversial readings, and, finally, about the status of the expression of divine will in the founding texts of Judaism.

Augustine identifies the diversity of languages with the "dissension" of souls. Outward history mirrors a different history, that of the transmission of the divine message, thus extending—thanks to the "translators"[2]—beyond the limits of its first appearance. The shift from an original language to several languages is symptomatic of a dual learning process, oriented both toward the original language and toward a particular language or languages. That cleavage is essential for Augustine, not only because it explains the difference between election and grace, between the Law and the Incarnation, but also because it legitimates the model of generalized conversion itself as the exclusive paradigm for religious and spiritual authenticity. The history of language and languages is also, in some sense, the history of Augustine himself.

"The Thing Is Neither Greek nor Latin"

In the first book of the *Confessions*, Augustine recounts that learning to speak is a movement from the darkness of forgetfulness to the intelligence of recognition and expression.[3] His account is instructive in that it serves as a model for the distinction between election and grace and sets in place the elements distinguishing Judaic reading from Christian:

> Later on I realized how I had learnt to speak. It was not my elders who showed me the words by some set system of instruction, in the way that they taught me to read not long afterwards; but, instead, I taught myself by using the intelligence which you, my God, gave to me. For when I tried to express my meaning by crying out and making various sounds and movement, so that my wishes should be obeyed, I found that I could not convey all that I meant or make myself understood by everyone

whom I wished to understand me. So my memory prompted me. I noticed that people would name some object and then turn towards whatever it was that they had named. I watched them and understood that the sound they made when they wanted to indicate that particular thing was the name which they gave to it, and their gestures clearly showed what they meant, for they are, as it were, the natural language of all men, consisting of expressions of the face and eyes, movements of other parts of the body, and also the tone of voice, which shows whether a person means to ask for something and get it, or refuse it and have nothing to do with it.[4]

Speech comes, in the first place, from observing and imitating, but already for the young Augustine it puts into play the distinction between spoken languages and a universal language (initially that of gestures). For the child, language also crystallizes the difficulty of expressing (but also of grasping) the will. This experience, both natural and fundamental, directs him, first, toward the necessary passage of the divine message through language, and second, toward the difficulties that such a passage raises regarding the sources and interpretation of that message.

The child begins to speak by imitating adults in order to express his wishes, to express himself. God will also speak the language of human beings, to give them the opportunity to be saved. Furthermore, God will take human form to save humankind. But fundamentally, the essential message, the truth of divine will, cannot be limited to the constraints of the word and of languages. Quite the contrary, and this is a decisive point in the Augustinian analysis: the divine message, like the intelligence given to the child by the Creator, is already present in the human being from the first act of creation.

Whereas gestures constitute the "natural language of all men," Christian revelation will be the agent of the universal and authentic language of humankind. It is the vehicle for the truth of the

Incarnation, a truth that transcends all language because it dwells in the memory and within human beings generally. A child learns through memory, but adulthood leads him to a paradoxical forgetfulness in his quest for happiness:

> Surely happiness is what everyone wants, so much so that there can be none who do not want it. But if they desire it so much, where did they learn what it was? If they have learnt to love it, where did they see it? Certainly happiness is in us, though how it comes to be there I cannot tell. . . . By some means or other they have learnt what it is. In some sense they have knowledge of it, and the problem before me is to discover whether or not this knowledge is in the memory. If it is, it means that at some time in the past we have been happy. . . . For we should not love happiness unless we knew what it was. We have heard it named and we all admit that it is our ambition to achieve it, for we do not take pleasure simply in the sound of the word. When a Greek hears it named in Latin, he derives no pleasure from it because he does not know what has been said. But we get pleasure from it, just as he would if he heard it spoken in Greek. This is because the thing is neither Greek nor Latin, but we are all eager to achieve it, whether we speak Greek or Latin or any other language. It must, then, be known to all.[5]

In the spiritual quest, language can become an obstacle because it locks a person inside a purely human communication, whereas truth appeals to a different language, that of memory and interiority. The child's confusion at his inability to express himself brings him into the social order, and the adult's confusion at the poverty of the language he speaks connects him to humankind in its pursuit of happiness. A forgetting of language, of one's own language, would seem to be the necessary condition for gaining access to what one is seeking and especially, for being able to rediscover the divine message.

That generalization (which in this context must even be called an "absolutization") of the economy of the Incarnation excludes election by its very principle. It does so because, according to Augustine, the truth, the true, is universal and needs no language, not even the language of Moses:

> Let me hear and understand the meaning of the words: In the Beginning you made heaven and earth. Moses wrote these words. He wrote them and passed on into your presence, leaving this world where you spoke to him. He is no longer here and I cannot see him face to face. But if he were here, I would lay hold of him and in your name I would beg and beseech him to explain those words to me. I would be all ears to catch the sounds that fell from his lips. If he spoke in Hebrew, his words would strike my ear in vain and none of their meaning would reach my mind. If he spoke in Latin, I should know what he said. But how should I know whether what he said was true? If I knew this too, it could not be from him that I got such knowledge. But deep inside me, in the dwelling of thought, Truth, which is neither Hebrew nor Greek nor Latin nor any foreign speech, would speak to me, though not in syllables formed by lips and tongue. It would whisper, "He speaks the truth."[6]

Grace, which for Augustine is the very truth of Christianity, lies beyond any language because it is addressed to the "dwelling of thought." That first "transcendence" of Judaism has an important companion in Augustine's thought, an element that informs his reception of election and his formulation of the oppositions and contrasts between the way of reading characteristic of the Law and that characteristic of grace. Before examining the texts in which Augustine focuses on the manifestation of the divine in the Old Testament, let us draw one last conclusion from his semiotic and linguistic analyses in the *Confessions*: Augustine's displacement of the site of truth to somewhere outside the field determined by the language of the first text allows him to establish a central methodological principle, that of the wholly legitimate possibility of relativizing the meaning of scripture in relation to the truth conveyed by the "dwelling of thought." Hence the Hebrew text becomes a translation into the reader's native tongue, shaped by him and by his perception of the truth of divine will:

> How can it harm me if I understand the writer's meaning in a different sense from that in which another understands it? All of us who read his words do our best to discover and understand what he had in mind, and since we believe that he wrote the truth, we are not so rash as to suppose that he wrote anything which we know or think to be false. Provided, therefore, that each of us tries as best he can to understand in the Holy Scriptures what the writer meant by them, what harm is there if a reader believes what you, the Light of all truthful minds, show him to be the true meaning? It may not even be the meaning which the writer had in mind, and yet he too saw in them a true meaning, different though it may have been from this.[7]

Reading, thus valorized, generalizes Old Testament prophecy, clearing a path for the narrative completion and fulfillment of the Old Testament in Christianity. The true reading, the one that gives access to the ultimate and true prophecy, results from an "assisted" reading. Its method is self-discovery, conveyed, for Augustine at any rate, through conversion: a return to interiority, to the place that makes it possible to see and decipher the divine message beyond the letter and intention of the text itself. "Moreover, not only among those who are called prophets, but in Old Testament history itself, one infers that prophecy [*Veteris Testamenti historia prophetia*] does not keep silent for those who seek devoutly and are aided by God in investigating these things [*et ad haec investiganda divinitus adjuvantur*]."[8]

The *Confessions* prepares the way for Augustine, pedagogue of Christianity, by opening the path to truth revealed by interiority. This first difference between the method of grace and that of election conceals many more. The Augustinian reader, propelled by his conception of truth, no longer has any need to master Hebrew or to consult the Greek. His intention, his point of view, and his perspective suffice to legitimate his interpretation. Since divine will is everywhere, it ultimately has no need for the first and original meaning of the text of scripture. The truth of divine will dispenses with languages, all languages, since it speaks the true language of interiority. The remedy for the "dissonance" created by the confusion of tongues resides not in a futile return to the original language, to a first divine language, but rather in the transcendence of all languages toward the absolute of interiority, the place to read both the self and divine will, and also the site of the human being's open availability, his expectation of grace. Within that context, Judaism represents only a first stage or manifestation of truth, its childhood (that figure will reappear in my discussion of Augustine's and Spinoza's philosophical legacy regarding election and grace). Like the child, election has constructed a language for itself in order to grasp and express the divine message, but it is a language that, for Augustine, calls for development, an extension and prolongation, and above all a completion, to achieve its hidden truth. Childhood both veils and anticipates adulthood. Similarly, election is only the first articulation of divine truth, that of the Incarnation and its grace.

Grace and the Ages of Humanity

Augustine's writings contain a great wealth of analyses and commentaries on the ages of humanity, their symbolism and theological meanings. To take one of the first commentaries on Genesis as a starting point: "The listing of the seven days and the presentation of their works is given a kind of conclusion, in which everything that has been said already is called *the book of the creating of heaven and earth* (Gn 2:4), even though it is only a small part of the book as a whole. But still it was entirely appropriate to give it this name, because these seven days furnish us with a miniature symbolic picture of the entire span of world history from start to finish."[9]

Necessarily linked to that exemplary role of the seven days (which will be considered again in the last book of the *City of God*,[10] in Augustine's discussion of the Creator's seventh day of rest) is the figure of the single man standing in for the entire history of humankind: "For, subject to the harmonious governance of all things by Divine Providence, the whole series of generations from Adam to the end of the world is administered as if it were the life of a single man who from boyhood through old age marks off the progress of his life into different age-levels."[11]

But even beyond these symbolic meanings, the three ages of humankind must be kept in mind, since they offer a framework, formulated in terms of the shift from the Law or election to grace:

> Seeing that the apostle Paul quite rightly says: "Before faith came, we were kept in custody under the Law" [Gal 3:23], the Lord also seems to mean this when he says of those whom he was going to feed the five loaves: "They did not need to go—you feed them" [Mt 14:16]. With these words they are figuratively detained, like those to be kept in custody, although the disciples had advised him to send them away [*Sub his autem verbis figuraliter tanquam custodiendi detinentur, cum hoc admonuissent discipuli, ut dimitteret eos*]. However, as for the multitude associated with the seven loaves, he felt a spontaneous pity for them, because it was already the third day since they had joined themselves to him in fasting, for, given the entire life span of the human race, this period in which the grace of Christian faith is given is the third period. The first is before the Law, the second, under the Law, and the third, under grace.[12]

The seven days are condensed here into a triad that is actually an overview of the history of humankind, but an overview that predicts the future of humanity: "The first phase is [our] activity prior to the Law; the second, under the Law; the third, under grace; and the fourth, in peace."[13]

Historical progress is punctuated by the shift toward grace and culminates in rest, as figured by the seventh day: a perfect narrative linearity and coherence, and an insistence on historical teleology that links the individual's fate to that of the human race, as a mark of both the authenticity and the truth of the allegory. For Augustine, scripture, when read correctly, is in some sense the biography of humankind, from the moment of its creation until its salvation. In that biography, it is imperative that we not let ourselves be held back or seduced by any one stage or period in particular. The intelligibility of the biography can be evaluated only on the basis of its conclusion, its end, its finality. Hence grace overtakes and outstrips election. Grace completes what remains unfinished under the Law, and Augustine sometimes compares that radical difference between the two orders to the difference between "conception" and birth, actualization: "There are therefore inchoate beginnings of faith, which resemble conception [*conceptionibus similes*]. It is not enough to be conceived. A man must also be born if he is to attain to eternal life. None of these beginnings is without the grace of God's mercy. And good works, if there are any, follow and do not precede that grace, as has been said."[14]

Grace completes what was only a conception under the Law. It "converts" election into its historical and eschatological finality. Augustine will translate and extend his model of conversion—with a privileged status given to self-reading as the guarantor of the authenticity of religious experience—to the collective body, the *Ecclesia*, and ultimately to the city and to humankind. In that way, the differences in order between the Law and the Incarnation, between grace and election, are expressed first as readability and visibility, the methods for deciphering speech and the image. The visible, like the image it sanctions, is only a reflection of divine choice, marked on the body as the site of its manifestation. For Augustine, reading and interpreting the "outer" surface as merely the expression of divine will amounts to a limitation, rooted in a misapprehension by the carnal senses of the powers and very nature of the divine. The external image is a seal, an imprint, a figure of what dwells deep within the human being. For Augustine, a confusion of images stands at the origin of the Jewish people's servitude, whereas Christian liberty [*christiana libertas*] is defined as a transcendence of the limits of signs and as an access to truth itself, a liberty that also makes access to the realities represented by word and image possible: "On this account Christian liberty [*christiana libertas*] freed those it found under useful signs, discovering them to be among those who were 'nigh,' interpreting the signs to which they were subject, and elevating them to the things which the signs represented. From them were constituted the Churches of the holy Israelites. For those it found under useless signs it not only prohibited and destroyed all servile obligation to those signs, but also destroyed the signs themselves."[15]

Christian liberty, resulting from an interpretation and a reading modeled on the conversion experience, stands opposed to the previous interpretive models and even goes so far as to call into question the very foundations of the truths of these interpretations.

The Dark Side of a Revelation That Is Not One

That Christian liberty finds expression, first, in the choice of a freedom to read that is in some sense a choice of allegory, despite Augustine's insistence on the "literal" reading in such works as *The Literal Meaning of Genesis*. The manner of reading confers an identity, especially in religious matters. According to Augustine, "when events are interpreted allegorically, they do not lose their historical value."[16] On the contrary, allegory, if it is coherent and constructed in keeping with the rules for properly reading scripture, constitutes the determining principle, the starting point for all interpretation, especially of the Old Testament: its figures, its prophecies, its visions, and its truths.[17]

In other words, human history is divided into several periods that follow an evolution organizing the divine order and revelation, and guiding the progress of humankind. In his questions to Simplician, Augustine slightly modifies that historical model to fit the context and nature of the difficulties the model is supposed to solve, difficulties that lie at the heart of the interpretation of the relation between grace and election. In place of a simple evolution or progress inscribed within the necessity of the Incarnation economy, this new version raises the problem of the nature and very function of the Law within that economy: "Therefore we must understand that the law was given not to introduce sin nor to extirpate it, but simply to make it known."[18]

That displacement could not be more significant, since it identifies the first function of the Law with that of an image, of the image: the Law shows and makes visible.[19] Because it makes visible what already exists, the Law is in some sense an occasion for sin. But although the Law is primarily an access route to the visibility of sin, for Augustine it nevertheless suffers, in its structure and its form, from a lack of God's visibility. It is as if, following a logic peculiar to Augustinian Christian "visibility," the Law, in making sin visible, does not allow one to see the ultimate truth and reality of God the Creator. Furthermore, the visibility that dwells within the Old Testament is essentially negative, since it cannot give direct access to divine will. Hence the importance, in this context, of Augustine's reflections on Old Testament visions and prophecies, on their modalities and material truth. That exploration of divine visibility in the Old Testament text pervades Augustine's entire oeuvre and addresses every possible detail of divine apparitions.

In the first place, there is the divine voice and its relation to the language spoken in paradise. What matters for our purposes is not the status of Hebrew as a divine language but rather whether any language at all was spoken by God. Initially, Augustine seems to hesitate between two possibilities:

> Again one may ask, in what way God now spoke to the man he made, who was already for sure endowed with sensation and intelligence, so that he would be capable of hearing and understanding. In no other way, after all, could he be a transgressor of the command received, unless he understood it when he received it. So in what way, then, did God speak to him? [*Quomodo ergo illi locutus est Deus?*] Was it inwardly in the mind, directly to his intelligence, that is so that he would clearly be aware of the command and understand God's will without any bodily sounds or likenesses of bodily things? But I do not somehow think that that is how God spoke to the first man. Scripture, I mean, is telling the sort of story which should lead us to suppose, rather, that God spoke to the man in Paradise just as he also spoke later on to the fathers, as he did to Abraham, as he did to Moses, that is, in some kind of bodily appearance. That, you see, is how they heard his voice as he took a stroll in Paradise towards evening and they then hid themselves.[20]

That first hesitation, formulated within the context of a demonstration of the possibility of a "literal" reading of the sacred text, will quickly be replaced by another explanation, closer to Augustine's final propensities and conceptions regarding the nature of revelation:

> Previously [perhaps] God used to talk to them in other interior ways, whether expressible in words or not, as he also talks to the angels, enlightening their minds with the unchangeable Truth itself; there understanding means knowing simultaneously

whatever things are happening in time and not simultaneously
. . . Now, however, [that apparition] . . . can only have been
effected visibly through some creature, lest that invisible substance of the Father and the Son and the Holy Spirit, which
is everywhere whole, should be supposed to have appeared to
their bodily senses by movement in time and space.[21]

Divine nature, in Augustine's view, does not lend itself to visibility. It does not offer itself to the gaze, except through representations and mediations, and it is these mediations that characterize, again according to Augustine, the order of the Law and of election. Before the visible apparition there is the voice, that of God or of his will. And the voice, as we know, suffers from the fragility of its ephemeral materiality; it lasts only the instant of the spoken word, it does no more than pass, leaving no traces or remainder behind, except perhaps in human memory, a memory vested by divine will. In fact, speech is what distinguishes the human being from his creator. Language marks the distinction between the human and the divine: on one hand, materiality, mutability, and disappearance; on the other, eternity and absolute presence. Because of that cleavage between the created and his creator, Augustine will erect the Word (a synonym for Christ) as an actualization of the Incarnation:

Who, after all, speaks in the way which the Word—*which was in the beginning with God* (Jn 1:1)—speaks? . . .
  Within you, my good man, when a word is in your heart, it is something other than a sound; but for the word which is in you to reach me, it seeks a sound as a vehicle. So it takes a sound, climbs somehow or other onto this vehicle, goes through the air, reaches me, and does not leave you. But for the sound to reach me, it did leave you, and did not remain with me. So then, the word which was in your heart did not go away when the sound went away, did it?

> You said what you were thinking, and for what was hidden in you to reach me, you put syllables together, in a sound; the sound of the syllables carried your thought to my ears, your thought climbed down through my ears into my heart, the sound which acted as intermediary flew away. But that word, which took on sound, was with you before you uttered it; because you did utter it, it is now with me and has not left you. Pay attention to that, whoever you are, you scrutinizer of sounds, you belittle the Word of God, you who do not understand the word of a human being![22]

For Augustine, the economy of the Incarnation requires a reassessment of all the divine apparitions in the Old Testament—a reassessment that, through his reading method, entails a Christian appropriation of the Hebrew text. Or, in other words, in examining the nature of these descriptions of divine apparitions in the Old Testament, Augustine relates them to the resumption, continuation, and completion of the limited visibility of election in the truth of grace. In effecting a transition from one era to the next, reading is in this case a calling into question:

> In those days there were many such manifestations, and though neither Father, Son, nor Holy Spirit was either named or unmistakably indicated in them, they still contained enough likely hints and probabilities to make it impossible without rashness to say that God the Father never appeared to the patriarchs or prophets under visible forms. This opinion stems from those people who could not recognize the unity of the Trinity in the words *To the king of ages, immortal, invisible and only God* (1 Tm 1:7) ... *whom no man has seen or can see* (1 Tm 6:16). But right-minded faith understands from these words the supreme and supremely divine and changeless substance in which the one and only God is at once Father and Son and Holy Spirit. All these visions, however, were produced through the changeable

creation subject to the changeless God, and they did not manifest God as he is in himself, but in a symbolic manner as times and circumstances required.[23]

The Old Testament thus offers only symbolic representations, fleeting figures inspired by the context and the place and fashioned to correspond to the circumstances of the time: partial apparitions in short, changing visions. After an overview of the key moments of the Old Testament, Augustine concludes:

> Accordingly, whatever it was that the Old Testament fathers saw whenever God showed himself to them, unfolding his plan of salvation in a manner suited to the times, it is clear that it was always achieved through created objects [*per creaturam facta esse manifestum est*]. . . . It is plainly stated in the letter to the Hebrews, where the author is distinguishing between the New Testament dispensation and the Old Testament dispensation, according to the requirements of different ages and times, that not only those visible phenomena of the Old Testament but also its verbal utterances were the work of angels [*Apertissime quippe scriptum est in Epistola ad Hebraeos, cum dispensatio Novi Testamenti a dispensatione Veteris Testamenti secundum congruentiam saeculorum ac temporum distingueretur, non tantum illa visibilia, sed ipsum etiam sermonem per Angelos factum*].[24]

Everything therefore proceeds, according to a plan formulated for the age of the Law and election, "through created objects." In a sense, Augustine devalorizes the revelations, visions, and miracles of the Old Testament by insisting on the modalities inscribed within the logic of the Incarnation economy and on the intelligibility of a recuperation of the Law within the specificity of Christian visibility. He does so with the aim of making a hypothesis, or a prejudice, inevitable. The partial visibility, as it were, of the Old Testament legitimates and accompanies the act of grace as the fulfillment of election. To take Augustine at his word, it is as if the Old Testament falls victim to the dark side of a revelation that is not truly one; or even to the misapprehension of the true nature of its revelation (a position similar to Spinoza's in the *Theological-Political Treatise*). Since Augustine's time, Judaism has continually been reproached for that misapprehension, a theological prejudice that gives rise to a method for reading the truth. The entire critique of the Judaic conception of election will proceed from that reproach or prejudice translated into truth, from that observation transformed into method and reading guide.

The economy of visibility mirrors the economy of grace and of election in the sense that, for Augustine, the "lapses" in the Old Testament or in its literal readings are expressed as an erroneous investment in election, in its modalities, and in its effects. Grace is quite simply the negation of the Jewish understanding of election, the establishment of a different conception of witnessing and of the role of the visible in revelation, and the recognition of the divine economy of the Incarnation. Hence,

> [the apostle's purpose] is that no man should glory in meritorious works, in which the Israelites dared to glory, alleging that they had served the law that had been given them, and that for that reason they had received evangelical grace as due to their merits. So they were unwilling that the same grace should be given to the Gentiles, as if they were unworthy of it unless they undertook to observe the Jewish sacred rites. This problem arose and is settled in the Acts of the Apostles [15]. The Jews did not understand that evangelical grace, just because of its very nature, is not given as a due reward for good works. Otherwise grace is not grace [Rom 11:6]. In many passages the apostle frequently bears witness to this, putting the grace of faith before works, not indeed that he wants to put an end to good works, but

to show that works do not precede grace but follow from it. No man is to think that he has received grace because he has done good works. Rather he could not have done good works unless he had received grace through faith.[25]

In some sense, grace is an antidote to the dangers of autonomy conveyed by election and also, according to Augustine, to the presumptuousness inaugurated by a certain valorization of election. Grace substitutes for election, introducing a new structure located outside any unfolding of history and beyond the constraints of Christian narrativity. Grace is still like election, except that it reinvents and redefines the role and status of bearing witness within the economy of the relationship between the human being and his God. Election inaugurates a temporality vested in and founded on a practice and a pragmatics of human history, on the realities of the world here below. But precisely because of its roots in human temporality, election is, at least for Augustine, only an agency for bearing witness; it is ultimately unsatisfying, temporary, and fleeting because public and collective, as well as fundamentally linked to an identity and a historical specificity. It bears witness not only to the covenant but also and above all to the visible and material signs of the distinctiveness of the chosen people, its difference from the rest of humankind. The distinction between election and grace also articulates the gap between the Law and faith, between what, on one hand, vests and authorizes visible signs, and what, on the other, is concealed in interiority, which for Augustine is the very site of the image.

Grace, in fact—and despite its effort to make visible what was hidden under and through the Law—dissimulates that act of bearing witness by internalizing it. It transforms bearing witness into a manifestation of the desire for submission to the divine gift, a desire itself inscribed not on visible and readable tablets but on a body and in the deepest recesses of the heart. In other words, grace brings about the transformation of signs and public images into an internal seal.

The Law confuses not only the image and the will but also merit and election. It sets in place an economy that, for Augustine, makes true grace superfluous, even useless:

> Are we to say that there could have been no election [*electio*] unless there had been, even when they were in their mother's womb, some difference of faith or works, or merit of some kind? But the apostle says, "That the purpose of God according to election [*electionem*] might stand." [Rom 9:11]. That is why we have to ask the question. Possibly we are to make a distinction here. Perhaps we should connect the words, "That the purpose of God according to election might stand," with what precedes rather than with what follows. It may mean not that the elder shall serve the younger *in order that* the purpose of God according to election may stand, but rather that children, who are not yet born and have done nothing, are given as an example that no election is here to be understood. If we read, "When they were not yet born and had done neither good nor evil, that the purpose of God according to election might stand" [Rom 9:11–12], it would mean that they had done neither good nor evil, so that there could be no election on account of his good deeds of the one who had done good. There could be no election on account of good works, according to which the purpose of God might stand. . . . So that the purpose of God does not stand according to election, but election is the result of the purpose of God [*non ergo secundum electionem propositum Dei manet, sed ex proposito electio*]. . . . Election does not precede justification, but follows it [*Non tamen electio praecedit justificationem, sed electionem justificatio*]. No one is elected unless he is different from him who is rejected. It is written that "God elected us before the foundation of the world" [*elegit nos Deus ante mundi constitutionem*] (Eph 1:4). I do not see how that could be except by way of foreknowledge. But here, when he says, "Not of works

but of him that calleth: [it was said unto her, The elder shall serve the younger]," he wants us to understand that it is not by election through merits, but by the free gift of God.[26]

The genesis of grace neutralizes the effects of election and introduces into the history of human society the primacy of a new economic order[27] founded on what Augustine calls "mutual transactions."[28] That new order is constituted by the circulation of the absolute gift and the expectation of its promise; it forges a reality that to a great extent neutralizes everything material, privileging the spiritual and the invisible, the mysterious and the secret. Grace as economy is the promise of a gift and the gift of anticipation. But it is also the mark of a new identity and of a new distinction, hidden and as it were sealed in the labyrinths of interiority. The universality of grace is derived from that inward-turning (not that election has overlooked interiority, but the Christian representation of election accuses it of doing so, by reducing election to the outward signs of its recognition). Grace makes the most of the translation of visibility into a new order, where bearing witness is the word and presence of the invisible itself: the Eucharist and the words *hoc est corpus meum* as body of interiority and mystery of the visibility of the mystery of the Incarnation.

Almost, or On Rereading As Religion

Before specifying a few of the forms of that internalization and the role they play in the grace/election dynamic, let us first ponder Augustine's hesitations about the realities and truths of Old Testament visions and miracles, since these hesitations reveal the keys to his method and its implications. In this context, the *Retractations* constitutes an irreplaceable source for discovering and following Augustine's concerns, in that it clarifies his thinking and revisits his writings.

Retractations is unique in its form and in its content. In this extraordinary book, Augustine, in rereading and sometimes correcting his own writings, performs a dual role. First, he asserts his authority (both as author and as doctor of the church) by identifying his works; and second, he proves himself to be an attentive and critical reader of his own texts. Hence this gesture, unique in Christian antiquity, is established through the critical practice of a rereading careful to explain expression as well as interpretation. In that sense, *Retractations* constitutes Augustine's most explicit legacy. Rereading, in this view, is not only a literary exercise, it is also a theological choice. Two examples will suffice.

The first has to do with *The City of God:* "In the tenth of these books, the following should not have been cited as a miracle: 'during the sacrifice of Abraham, a fire enkindled in heaven ran between the separated victims,' for this was shown to him in a dream."[29] The dream, like the voice and visions, like writing and signs, like all that is ephemeral and marked by passing, is suspect. The divine reveals itself through these mediations only partially, barely at all.

The second example refers to a passage from "Answer to Adimantus":

> In this book I said: "For before the coming of the Lord, the people who had received the Old Testament were sustained by certain shadowy signs and figures according to a wonderful and well ordered arrangement of the times; in it, however, there is such an announcement and preparation of the New Testament that in the Gospel and in the teaching of the Apostles no precepts and promises, howsoever difficult and divine, are found which are not also found in those ancient books." But I should have added the word, "almost," and then it would read that "in the Gospel and in the teaching of the Apostles *almost* no precepts and divine promises are found which are not also found in those ancient books." For what is the meaning of the words of the Lord in the Sermon on the Mount in the Gospel: "You have heard that this was said to the ancients; . . . but I say to you" [Mt

5:21–22], if He Himself does not enjoin anything more than was enjoined in those ancient books? Furthermore, we do not read that "the kingdom of heaven" was promised to that people among the things that were promised by the Law given by Moses on Mount Sinai which is properly called the Old Testament and which the Apostle says was prefigured by the handmaid of Sara and her son. But the New Testament is also prefigured there by Sara herself and her son. Accordingly, if figures are examined, all things that have been prophesied which have been realized or are expected to be realized by Christ are found there. But, nevertheless, because of certain precepts, not prefigured but real, which are found not in the Old but in the New Testament, I should have said more circumspectly and more carefully "almost no" rather than "no" [precepts and promises] are here. Moreover, there are there (i.e. in the Old Testament) the two precepts of love of God and neighbor whereby everything concerning the Law, the Prophets, the Evangelists, and the Apostles is most rightly connected.[30]

For Augustine, everything plays out around one word: *almost*, which marks the difference and names what, in Christianity, gives voice to the Jewish Bible. *Almost* thus puts on display the shadow of a relic, tracing the multiple paths of appropriation and recuperation in the wake of a problematic rooted in the relationship between what is said and what has not been wholly understood, between what is partially visible, what is sayable, and what is revealed through reading. *Almost* names the method outlined in the *Confessions* and perfected throughout Augustine's career, that way of reading with and against the text and its author, and admirably expresses the relation between the letter and the spirit, between election and grace, between the synagogue and the church. Such, in brief, is Augustine's method.

We are justified in wondering about the reason for that last hesitation, that final desire for precision, in a discourse that on the whole remains the same and that, moreover, advances and elucidates the logic behind and arguments for appropriating the Old Testament. Perhaps we should see it as a rhetorical flourish, a ruse, whose ultimate aim would be to always refer back to the details, to the vicissitudes of the narratives, to their detours. Is it an invitation to apply the Augustinian method of reading and interpreting the visions and manifestations of God in the Old Testament, as well as the true method for reading the revealed text, to Augustine's own texts? It may be from that standpoint that we should attempt to understand his insistence on the relation between religion and reading. In that sense the *Retractations*, as its modern editors say, reveals "Saint Augustine's soul," that is, his ultimate text, his last word on Christian truth and its relation to the legacy of Old Testament election.[31]

Augustine goes so far as to identify religion with reading, Christianity with reading. Hence the choice Augustine speaks of is both election and conversion. It is a reading of oneself and a rereading of the world:

> It is that we may see Him, so far as He can be seen; it is that we may cleave to Him, that we are cleansed from all stain of sins and evil passions, and are consecrated in His name. For He is the fountain of our happiness, He the end of all our desires. In choosing Him, or rather let me say, in rechoosing him [*Hunc eligentes vel potius religentes*] [from which, it is said, comes the word for religion, *religio*]—for we had lost Him through our neglect—[we] may rest in Him, and find our blessedness by attaining that end.[32]

Apart from the debates concerning the etymology of the word *religio*, Augustine's text is revealing in more ways than one: it offers us the culminating point and synopsis of his thinking on Christian faith as election or choice and reading, as a voluntary act of submission to the order of grace. And, in so doing, it gives us an idea of the motives behind his *reading* of the Law and of election. According to

Augustine, then, Christianity is an act of rereading, a rereading of the Old Testament, just as grace is a rereading of election, a rereading of oneself after conversion, and a rereading of history through the choice of grace. Everything is therefore return and repetition, a displacement toward a new context whose intelligibility depends in great part on its ability to continue, resume, and complete what preceded it. Rereading is a movement toward plenitude, an orientation toward totality, a path toward the origin. Augustine's methodological treatises (from "On Genesis—A Refutation of the Manichees" to *The Literal Meaning of Genesis* and *The Trinity*, not to overlook the *Confessions*) thus incarnate, in their very practice, that desire to identify religious experience with the act of reading, and more precisely, with the practice of rereading: rereading of self as the first step toward rereading the tradition; rereading of election in grace.

Indeed, it is tempting to say that Christianity, in contrast to Judaism, is itself a "retractation" in the Augustinian sense of the term and that, for Augustine, Judaism is only a *pre-text*, a prior text as it were, that receives its meaning and true significance only with its Christian negation, in the determining act of its definitive rereading. That rereading, by rejecting the reality of a direct revelation in the Old Testament, privileges the need for an interpretive method that plumbs the secrets of mediation and the mysteries of their manifestations under the Law. That rereading therefore establishes a new tradition whose aim is to preserve and transmit the signs of the proper reading or rereading. A new genealogy is built on the questioning of the genesis of the reception and transmission of Old Testament truths: rupture and continuity, a quest for origins by virtue of the need to recognize disputed ancestors.

Augustine the pedagogue, evoked at the beginning of this chapter, is Augustine pure and simple: in his writings, everything seems to turn on reading or rereading, in all the weight he grants that term.

The founding gesture of this Augustinian conception of religion lies in the systematic rejection of any real direct revelation of the divine in the Old Testament, whether that means the voice of God, his image, his epiphanies, or even his will. Everything is now mediation, everything representation. It is tempting to see that position as a transformation and radicalization of one of the major aspects of the Manichaean attitude toward the Old Testament. He would therefore move surreptitiously from the refutation of the revelation of the Evil God to the out-and-out negation of the direct presence of God the Creator himself. What remains, and it is a legacy whose enormous burden continues to stir up contemporary debates on the relation between Judaism and Christianity, is a genealogy recuperated through the difficult and contested paths of mediation and transmission. The narrative closure constitutive of Christianity is a way of reading, a way of seeing; ultimately, it is a saying of what was never said or seen as such in the Old Testament. It is a reading informed by what will come to pass. Thus, for example, the visibility of the Incarnation is known through its invisibility in Old Testament dreams and visions. The same is true for grace: it is inscribed in election while being, at the same time, misapprehended. For that reason Augustine continually repeats, even against the Manichaeans, that the Law cannot and must not be abrogated. It must rather be better understood: "The Jews did not understand the observance of the Sabbath. . . . That passage of scripture signifies this Sabbath, that is, this rest, which the Jews did not understand. . . . The Lord, then, did not rescind the scripture of the Old Testament, but he makes us understand it [*Non ergo Dominus rescindit scripturam Veteris Testamenti, sed cogit intelligi*]; nor did he undo the Sabbath so that what was prefigured would be lost, but rather he reveals it so that what was hidden might be seen."[33]

Christ is thus conceived in the same terms as those characterizing the Christian's choice: as the quest for true meaning, for what is hidden behind the veil of the figures of the Law.

> For the Son himself, that is, the Word of God, not only in the last times when he deigned to appear in the flesh but even

earlier, from the creation of the world, made the Father known to whom he willed, whether by speaking or by appearing, either through some angelic power or through just any creature. He is, after all, the truth in all things; all things exist for him, and all things obey the least sign from him and are subject to him, so that he is seen by whom he chooses, when he wants to be seen, through a visible creature, even with their eyes. And yet, according to his divinity and insofar as he is the Word of the Father, coeternal with the Father and immutable, through whom all things are made, he is seen only by a heart that has been completely purified and is utterly simple. . . . But whether it was in the bush when God sent him or later when he gave [Moses] the law, Stephen says in the Acts of the Apostles that an angel appeared to [Moses]. We say this so that no one might suppose that the Word Of God, by whom all things were made, can be limited as if by locality and can visibly appear to someone otherwise than through some visible creature.[34]

That explanation—against the Manichaeans—retraces the same arguments Augustine develops to explain both the nature of the Old Testament and the status of divine apparition under the Law. In this context, it is possible to follow an important shift in Augustine's attitude vis-à-vis his former confreres, who rejected the Old Testament as the creation of the Prince of Darkness and who even suspected the New Testament of having been corrupted.[35] Instead of claiming the corruption or evil origin of the Old Testament, Augustine softens his analysis, insisting on the modalities of divine presence in the text and especially on ways of reading it so as to interpret it properly.

Revision, rereading, and return to self: such are the founding gestures of that Augustinian Christianity, of its city and its order. The Christian city, that of grace, finds its origin in a choice or, more precisely, in an *election* that is only the choice of grace and its modalities. Christian universality is thus affirmed through the choice made by an individual, through an assertion of individual will. In place of the covenant, which was the mark of distinction and separation between a people and the rest of the world, Augustine renders the order of grace as universal submission brought about by introspection, the examination of conscience, in short, by generalized confession. Grace, then, replaces the chosen people with humankind. That universalization is a generalization rooted not in a reformulation or a rereading of divine will—which for Augustine takes concrete form by turning the covenant and election on their heads—but in individual initiative. With Christianity, it is the individual who must choose God; it is the human being who must recognize nature, his own nature, in order to be able to turn toward God. An individual choice, the individual's choice: a perfect resemblance between the true order of grace and that of the Incarnation. In each case, a new intermediary is chosen. For Augustine, that choice avoids the problems and disadvantages arising with the apparitions of divinity in the Old Testament. In the shift from prophecy to the Incarnation and from election to grace, the essential relationship between God and his creature is redefined and reformulated.

Augustine goes so far as to identify, under the order of the Law and covenant, precise signs and traces of misapprehended grace. He will identify a flawless continuity from the origin, a continuity, it goes without saying, that is misapprehended:

> *Death reigned from Adam until Moses* (Rom 5:14), since the law given through Moses could not overcome it. The law was not, after all, given in order to be able to bestow life [Gal 3:21]. Rather, the law was meant to show that the dead, for whose restoration to life grace was needed, were not only laid low by the propagation and dominion of sin, but also found guilty in addition by transgression of the law. This was not so that anyone who, even at that time, understood in the light of God's mercy should perish; it was rather, so that those destined for

punishment through the reign of death might come to know themselves for what they are by transgressing the law and seeking God's help. Thus *where sin abounded, grace was even more abundant* (Rom 5:20), and this grace alone sets one free *from the body of this death* (Rom 7:24–25).

Although the law given through Moses could not remove from anyone the reign of death, there were, nonetheless, at the time of the law men and women of God, not living under the law that terrifies, convicts, and punishes, but under grace that delights, heals, and sets free.[36]

Such is the paradox of the economy of grace. Grace is the gift of a law that makes visible, that shows; and, by that very fact, the law is evacuated of the authenticity and veracity of its own images. A transitional law therefore. A temporary law, a sign that, like any material sign, has, so to speak, a residue, a remainder, even when it is supposed to yield its place to what it represents. Although grace is the fullness of the Law, the Law persists and sets in place a different economy of divine revelation. In that sense, salvation and election are in conflict, opposition even. The opposition between the two, conveyed here through the contrast between terror and delight, and through the distance between submission (conviction) and freedom, ultimately encompasses the entire distance between the two orders, that of election and that of grace. For Augustine, grace "delights" [*gratia delectante*] because it is an absolute and unexpected gift that need not be returned or reciprocated, whereas the Law is founded on a mutual relationship, on an exchange and an expectation.

Grace, like the Incarnation, constitutes Christian specificity, a redefinition of human nature and a "new" identification of the modalities of divine action. Whereas election, at least in its Christian version, designates a collective selection and choice, grace is general and individual at the same time. It is marked by a different conception of freedom, by a form of availability, a continual receptivity to a possibility and a promise. Hence the importance in Augustine's writing of what look to us like hesitations, reconsiderations that indicate a desire for both methodological and theological precision, accuracy, and above all coherence.

The manifestations of divine presence—their variations—are a sign or rather a figure of an impossibility, of an unthinkability for someone determined to grasp and describe the relation between the Incarnation and grace. The generalization of the model of conversion as self-reading, as return to self, that is, as rediscovery and reunion, completes the appropriation of the legacy of election. And that rediscovery and reunion come about not only through interiority but also through a necessity that defines and characterizes human nature by means of its relation to the divine, its openness, by means of its availability to a divine veiled writing that has remained partly unknown, forgotten, and even misapprehended.

Conversion does not identify human nature with God's nature: it transforms human nature into a partial, incomplete, unfinished image of the divine. It opens the way to a possible completion by and through self-reading. It is, quite simply, an act of grace, a spiritual ruse whose *kairos* is a conversion or a rereading and, in that precise sense, a re-election.

Conversion thus constitutes itself as a dual turning or dual movement that combines will and grace, image and mystery, voice and authenticity, presence and recognition.

"We Are God's Coinage"

Whereas election results from the covenant and the contract that covenant establishes between God and his chosen people, Christianity proposes a different contract, one that mirrors the specificity of the Incarnation and the visibility proper to it.[37] It is within that context that we are to understand the monetary and economic metaphors that abound in Augustine's descriptions of the nature of the bond between God and his people. It is noteworthy that the new Christian contract is nothing other than the symbol, or creed, which functions as the economic realization or actualization of the new reality. The symbol too is a model of exchange, a contract, and, in its Augustinian version, it incarnates all the modalities required by the order of grace. It is, at first sight, a new covenant: "We have made a pact and agreement [*pactum et placitum*] with God, and put our signature in the bond to a condition for the canceling of the debt."[38]

The exchange between the believer and his God obeys the laws of debt, of mutual acknowledgment, and thus requires that the believer come forward and pledge himself as a bond.[39] But that gift and that self-renunciation call for reciprocity, an other. They also presuppose a witness and a material support. Augustine reminds us that the word "symbol" was "transferred from commercial transactions, because merchants make agreements among themselves, called symbols, which guarantee their loyalty to the terms of their association. And your association is concerned with spiritual merchandise so that you may be like *dealers looking for a good pearl* (Mt 13:45). The pearl is *the charity, which will be poured out in your hearts through the Holy Spirit, who will be given to you.*"[40] The symbol represents an exchange, an agreement, which implies the potential for a restoration; it is a partition and a division that await a future return and reunification. That relation to a future promise is characteristic of the Christian symbol; the promise gives the symbol its identity and distinguishes it from the Law, by orienting the symbol toward the gift of grace. Moreover (to recall Benveniste's analyses of the connection between credit and faith, between the economic and the religious),[41] the Augustinian symbol constitutes a community that, by virtue of its origin and nature, does not allow for any identity-based autonomy like that characterizing the collectivity constituted by election.[42] Is election a self-affirmation and a self-possession, or, on the contrary, a strategy of separation, not to say of exclusion? The Augustinian reading suggests that the symbol, icon of the order of grace, is the foundation of a new temporality constitutive of the new community, where the play between gift and debt governs the operation and organization of both the social and the spiritual. That political dimension of the Augustinian city continually negotiates between the privilege of interiority and the need for institutional structures and forms of government for the collectivity, two aspects that stand in an essential tension with each other. That negotiation is a consequence not only of grace and its privileges but also of the desire to neutralize what is specifically historical in the Jewish legacy.

The symbol has a privileged connection to memory. As a result, it must not be set down in writing. According to Augustine, it must always remain something like a sermon, a promise, or a spoken exchange. It is as if writing, the materiality of inscribed words, incurred the risk of diminishing the symbol's value and power. Writing would distance the believer from the words, which must circulate and stir his heart through his continuous meditation on (we might even say rereading of) their significance. The symbol, then, is also reserved for the conscience, that mysterious place that for Augustine is the dwelling of thought. Like a summation, the symbol stands in for the whole truth of scripture:

> So now, I have paid my debt to you with this short sermon on the whole Symbol. When you hear the whole of this Symbol, you will recognize this sermon of mine briefly summed up in it. And in no way are you to write it down, in order to retain the same words; but you are to learn it thoroughly by hearing it, and not write it down either when you have it by heart, but keep it always and go over it in your memory. After all, everything you are going to hear in the Symbol is already contained in the divine documents of the holy scriptures, from which you regularly hear extracts as the need arises.
>
> But the fact that the Symbol, put together and reduced to a certain form in this way, may not be written down, is a reminder

of God's promise, where he foretold the new covenant through the prophet, and said, *This is the covenant which I will draw up for them after those days, says the Lord; putting my laws into their minds, I will write them also on their hearts* [*et in cordibus eorum scribam eas*] (Jer 31:33).[43]

This new economy and new writing are symbolized by new surfaces; at least for Augustine, the shift from the old to the new is symbolized by the displacement from the viscera or belly to the heart. But what matter are the figures and places of inscription, and the models of exchange they make possible. "You regularly hear . . . as the need arises": the context determines how the text and its message are to be understood. The symbol sets in place an economy of the spoken word that describes and legitimates the relationship between God and the individual, between God and his people.

To assess the importance of that explanation of the symbol, we have only to compare it to that of Ambrose of Milan who, in his *Treatise on the Symbol*, also emphasizes that the text must never be written down:

> Take heed of this: the symbol must not be written down. For you have to render it, but let no one write it down. For what reason? We have received it in such a way that it must not be written down. What must you do? Keep it. But you will say: How can we keep it if we do not write it down? For what reason? Here it is. Anything you write down, because you are sure you will be able to reread it, you do not apply yourself to going over [*recensere*] it every day, meditating on it. Conversely, what you do not write down, you are afraid of forgetting, and you apply yourself to going over [*recensere*] it every day. And that is a great help. Your soul and body grow sluggish, the enemy who never sleeps tempts you, your body becomes agitated, you have a bellyache: go over [*recense*] the symbol, and you will be healed. Go

over [*recense*] it in yourselves, especially in yourselves. Why? So that you do not acquire the habit, by repeating it too loudly apart from you, where there are faithful, of applying yourself to going over [*recensere*] it among the catechumens or heretics."[44]

Here the symbol is a silent, active speech that has the power to heal and guide. But Augustine, while retaining that essential function of the symbol, highlights the collective and political dimension: it is the gift of the New Testament, a gift that puts surfaces and prophecies into play as marks of the difference between the old and the new, election and grace.

That return to interiority has another function: to distinguish categorically between election and grace, between the Law and the symbol. "Such are they of whom the . . . apostle speaks as 'being ignorant of God's justice, and wishing to establish their own justice, who have not submitted themselves to the justice of God' [Rom. 10:3]. He said this of the Jews, who in their self-assumption rejected grace, and therefore did not believe in Christ. Their own justice, indeed, he says, they wish to establish; and this justice is of the law—not that the law was established by themselves, but that they had constituted their justice in the law which is of God, when they supposed themselves able to fulfil that law by their own strength, ignorant of God's justice—not indeed that by which God is himself just, but that which man has from God."[45]

In Augustine's analysis, the Law, though founded on a gift from God, remains a human law because it overlooks and misapprehends, or worse, because it refuses, the other, more fundamental gift of grace. Two economies stand opposed—two ways of being available and of organizing one's life at the individual and collective levels—based on the justice they establish: on one hand, human justice, stemming from a divine origin but ultimately detached from it; on the other, God's true justice. For Augustine, at any rate, the contrast between the two models defines the essential difference between the two communities, between their laws, their governments, and their destinies. The Hebrew model is forever marked by a stubborn choice, an admirable but blind devotion, a desire for separation; the Christian model aspires to be universal and sees election as only a temporary state, a way station on the path to salvation. The Law, with the misapprehension lying behind it, is for Augustine an abandonment of God. It takes shape as a movement that distances the human being from his creator and that, as a result, unfolds as a rejection of grace and of the "conversion" that accompanies it. It is the principal model for the city here below, founded on purely human laws and conventions, without any knowledge or acknowledgment of grace at all. The application of the Law, or, more accurately, the *desire* for the application of the Law, which lies at the origin of that separation—that forgetting of grace—designates the difference between the Christian, who is open and available to grace, and the rest of humankind. The will that recognizes God and not simply his Law corresponds to grace and its gifts. Without that dual movement, no true connection between God and his creature is possible. For Augustine, in any case, wishing to carry out the Law is equivalent to taking one's distance from God. It inaugurates the distance and alienation that grace alone can eliminate.

Nothing represents that alienation better than the intimate connection between the Law and reason:

> Whether we mean natural law, which appears when a person reaches the age at which he is capable of using reason, or the written law, which was given through Moses, it was not able on its own to give life and set us free *from the law of sin and death* (Rom. 8.2), which was contracted from Adam. . . . Hence, since there is also a law in the reason of a human being who already uses free choice, a law naturally written in his heart, by which he is warned that he should not do anything to anyone else that he himself does not want to suffer, all are transgressors

according to this law, even those who have not received the law given through Moses.[46]

This remarkable text brings to mind certain passages from Spinoza's *Theological-Political Treatise*, and encapsulates the difficulties of associating human reason with an interpretation of the Law founded on the primacy of election, difficulties that allude to the shift from the local to the universal in the advent of the order of grace.

Surfaces: From the Viscera to the Heart

Nature inscribes its law in the human heart, and the Creator writes his will on the same surface. The difference between election and grace can be expressed as the nature of the surface on which the law is inscribed and received, the very materiality of that support. The evolution can be summed up quite simply as an elevation toward the heart, a progression from the "viscera," the belly, to the repository of divine will. Indeed, Augustinian interiority, in the wake of Paul, is also a surface and a materiality in which a covenant is inscribed and a community is formed, a community characterized by the nature of its relation to the divine in its material manifestations. Within that framework, the shift from election to grace attests to a shift from the viscera to the heart, the absolute symbol of the most profound, the most intimate, interiority. The object of inscription, the very nature of that inscribed surface and its substantiality, and its appearance or invisibility, are so many marks designating the modalities of an inaugural institution, a foundation both spiritual and political. That divine writing announces a future, which for Augustine is that of the order of grace. "[The Lord] wrote on the earth when he bent down to the earth; before bending down to the earth he had written not on earth but on stone. The earth began to be fruitful, for it was to bring forth its abundance when sown with the letters of the Lord. Of old he had written the law on stone to signify this hard-heartedness of the Jews; now he wrote on earth, to signify the fertility of Christians."[47]

This contrast between Christians and Jews is, of course, shaped in good part by the Pauline texts. It seems to me, however, that it is also inscribed in a specifically Augustinian problematic formulated throughout the *Homilies on the Gospel of John*, which refers to problems of speech, its structure and materiality, and to the way it makes necessary a form of internal writing, the only kind capable of receiving and retaining the divine message. The distinction between Christianity and Judaism will be articulated in terms of differences in the nature of the word, setting the covenant against the symbol, election against grace.

This transcendence of the covenant and its historical context, this would-be passing beyond the boundaries (geographical, cultural, linguistic, ideational) of the specificity of Jewish history, opens the way to the universality of Christian revelation. Election, in this context, is reduced to a moment in an evolution, an inevitable progression, and is predicted in the texts of the covenant itself. Grace *converts* election because, for Augustine, it restores election's true meaning.

Conversion, as the paradigmatic model of religious authenticity, introduces a new mode of bearing witness, a new modality for articulating and displaying faith. In this case, Augustine's writings are both exemplary and remarkable—almost unique—because they give Christianity, his Christianity, an unparalleled doctrinal coherence, a vocabulary and a language that at every moment connect the particular, the individual, to the collective and doctrinal. God no longer addresses a people or even his chosen people: he now speaks to man in general, to a particular man and to all men. Jeremiah says that the Law is put in the inward parts, the viscera, but is written in the heart ("I will put their law in their inward parts, and write it in their hearts; and will be their God, and they shall be my people"—Jer 31:33, KJV). For Augustine, everything turns on that place or site of the Law, be it the viscera or the reason.[48]

These viscera, sign and name for an interiority that is utterly carnal according to Augustine, will be replaced by an entirely spiritual economy, that of the heart, its surface, and above all its language. That internal language, both silent and absolute, requires continuous introspection, a repeated examination of conscience, a practice of generalized conversion.

If, as Augustine says, Moses writes his law and passes on, who will read the Law, and how are they to seek and find its truth? It is through the act of writing that reading is actualized and externalized: Augustine's own writing in the first place, and especially his autobiography. As Pierre Courcelle has noted, the *Confessions* is "in a sense . . . one of those lists of sins that Saint Antony the Great recommended be set down in writing."[49] In fact, Athanasius's *Vita Antonii* is a major model for Augustine in the *Confessions*, especially for everything having to do with the role of reading and writing. Here is the passage in which Antony recommends writing:

> Now daily let each one recount to himself his actions of the day and night. . . . And may this remark serve as a precaution so that we might not sin: Let each one of us note and record our actions and the stirrings of our souls as though we were going to give an account to each other. And you can be sure that, being particularly ashamed to have them made known, we would stop sinning and even meditating on something evil. For who wants to be seen sinning? Or who, after sinning, would not prefer to lie, wanting it to remain unknown? So then, just as we would not practice fornication if we were observing each other directly, so also we will doubtless keep ourselves from impure thoughts, ashamed to have them known, if we record our thoughts as if reporting them to each other. Let this record replace the eyes of our fellow ascetics, so that, blushing as much to write as to be seen, we might never be absorbed by evil things. Patterning ourselves in this way, we shall be able to

enslave the body, as well as please the Lord and trample on the deceptions of the enemy.[50]

Writing replaces the eye: it is a witness and introduces the model of confession itself into the daily examination of conscience. Writing, according to Antony, purifies the heart and makes it possible to master the passions and the body. The externalization of thought, its representation and materialization through writing, bring into being a virtual public space that, within the context of the spiritual exercise, transforms self-control into a collective, social practice. That practice gives a rough idea of all the power and efficacy of the confession exploited by Augustine. "I need not tell all this to you, my God, but in your presence I tell it to my own kind, to those other men [*cui narro haec? neque enim tibi, deus meus, sed apud te narro haec generi meo, generi humano*], however few, who may perhaps pick up this book. And I tell it so that I and all who read my words may realize the depths from which we are to cry to you. Your ears will surely listen to the cry of a penitent heart which lives the life of faith."[51]

Whereas writing, according to Antony, purifies the heart by standing in for the other's gaze, Augustine's writing addresses humankind as a whole. In addition, God is Augustine's witness in his effort to recount and confess his life. It is also important to note that Augustine emphasizes the cry and the ear, privileging the audible and the sonorous over the written and inscribed. How to explain this displacement, especially when we know of Augustine's reticence concerning anything related to the voice and its fragility? The displacement comes about because, for Augustine, the Father reveals himself through the voice.[52] Augustine's consideration of the voice, it seems to me, distances him from Saint Paul's problematic of writing on and in the heart, and from his models of the difference between Judaism and Christianity. Here it is the Gospel of John, with the central status granted to the Word, the Logos, that informs Augustine's commentary on the Trinity and the Incarnation conveyed through the image and the heart's ear.

> The sounds, that is, which issue from your mouth, and by lashing the air in between strike the ears of your son, and by filling his sense of hearing bring your thought to his heart; those sounds, then, are not you yourself, are not your son himself. A sign has been given by your spirit to your son's spirit, and the sign is neither your spirit nor your son's spirit, but something else.
>
> Are we to suppose that the Father spoke with the Son in that way? Did words pass between God and the Word? How did that happen? If the Father wished to say something to the Son, if he wanted to say it with a word, well, the Son is the Word of the Father; would he ever use a word to speak to the Word? Or because the Son is the Word par excellence [*magnum Verbum*], were lesser words [*minora verba*] going to run back and forth between Father and Son?[53]

At this point, election seems to have been forgotten: everything occurs within the Trinity, among its members. And the human being, for his salvation, is invited to turn inward and rediscover his internal ears and eyes. The Incarnation opens the era to the Word, the Logos, and with it, at any rate for Augustine, to the Word of conversion (of the individual, of humankind, and of the Law and its election), which necessarily passes through the intermediary of writing and reading in the form of confession. Augustine's writings on grace are haunted by a constant need to justify the recuperation of the Law within the economy of the Incarnation, a concern that proceeds by spiritualizing speech, by locating it in the invisibility of interiority. For our purposes, the importance of the texts Augustine devotes to the Gospel of John lies in their explanation of the structure of the Trinity in terms that shape the possible communication between the believer and his creator. The voice and the heart, like the internal gaze and the cry, are in this case keys to the religious experience. These formulations of faith and of its reality, moreover, will be adapted, modified, and often critiqued by Spinoza and his readers.

The commentaries on John repeat, in practical terms, the lessons and conclusions of *The Trinity* concerning the nature of Old Testament theophanies: "Even if [God] appeared in visible or audible fashion, it was through the intermediary of the creature and not in his own proper substance [*non per substantiam*]. To see that substance, hearts have to be purified by all these things which are seen by eyes and heard by ears."[54]

The Augustinian study of Old Testament theophanies concludes with the acknowledgment of an impossibility, that of direct divine manifestation. What Augustine develops, in contrast, is a method that consists of seeing the divine behind what he often calls the "intermediary of the creature," a method that, in appealing to the heart, addresses humankind as a whole, thus neutralizing the supposedly exclusive Hebrew election and its privileges.

Cities

The universality of Christianity, in its complex relation to its rivals, is not limited to Judaism, however. Augustine devotes a section of *The City of God* to critiquing paganism, its gods and its cults. The city and the republic, as a social and political structure, are at the heart of the Augustinian critique of Roman paganism. Within the context of his analyses of the bonds that constitute and, as it were, make the city, he privileges the notion of justice as an evaluative criterion. That justice certainly brings to mind the *christiana beata* we have already encountered in the Augustinian critique of election and of the Law. Augustine's method is almost the same in both cases: he seeks to prove that behind the pagan conception of justice lurks a contradiction, an impossibility. The demonstration is impressive because it introduces the concept of Christianity into the very heart of paganism, just as

Augustine had already presented the Incarnation as the truth of the Old Testament. Here the order of grace transforms the polis and its politics as well as justice, and ultimately transforms the social bond itself. "This, then, is the place where I should fulfil the promise I gave in the second book of this work, and explain, as briefly and clearly as possible, that if we are to accept the definitions laid down by Scipio in Cicero's *De Republica*, there never was a Roman republic; for he briefly defines a republic as the thing of the people [*Breviter enim rempublicam definit esse rem populi*]. And if this definition be true, there never was a Roman republic."[55]

As we already knew, the thing is neither Greek nor Latin nor Hebrew. And now, it seems, the political thing cannot be Latin or Greek. At the foundation of Augustine's argument (but is it truly an argument or merely an assertion of the primacy of the theological in political matters?), we find justice and accuracy [*justice et justesse*]: the accuracy of the Ciceronian definitions of the people and of the city; and the justice implied in the definition of the people and the "thing of the people." The stakes are enormous, since, for Augustine at any rate—and the same problem will be found later in Spinoza— they include the legitimacy and cohesion of a community, of any community, and the nature of the social bond. Augustine constructs his indictment of Cicero's republic in the form of a pyramid, with justice at its apex:

> For the people, according to [Scipio's] definition, is an assemblage associated by a common acknowledgment of right and by a community of interests. And what he means by a common acknowledgment of right he explains at large, showing that a republic cannot be administered without justice. . . . For the unjust inventions of men are neither to be considered nor spoken of as rights; for even they themselves say that right is that which flows from the fountain of justice, and deny the definition which is commonly given by those who misconceive the

matter, that right is that which is useful to the stronger party. Thus, where there is not true justice there can be no assemblage of men associated by a common acknowledgment of right ... and if [there be] no people, then no thing of the people, but only of some promiscuous multitude unworthy of the name.[56]

Augustine's verdict is absolute: neither people nor thing of the people; neither republic nor justice. The world of paganism suffers from a confusion similar in some sense to that of languages, but in the case of paganism it is rather a confusion of definitions, of categories, and of notions, a misapprehension of true justice and a blindness to the signs of its presence. Cicero's republic, with everything it entails and implies, is undermined by an internal contradiction, pervaded by a profound ignorance that makes it a purely imaginary and fictive entity. What is missing, what is lacking, is "the justice whereby the one supreme God rules the obedient city according to His grace, so that it sacrifices to none but Him, and whereby, in all the citizens of this obedient city, the soul consequently rules the body and reason the vices in the rightful order, so that, as the individual just man, so also the community and people of the just, live by faith, which works by love."[57]

Here again are all the main threads of the Augustinian theme of grace: the equivalence between the individual and humankind; the superiority of grace, given its penetration into all dimensions of human life, of the body, even the soul; and salvation.

Grace Christianizes the city, inaugurates its polis and especially its politics. Hence the earthly city is a city of grace, with the justice and promise of grace. And the "chosen" are those subject to that gift, not those who identify themselves and join together either through a covenant or through mutual consent about human justice or through any other accord or contract. From that perspective, Augustine, in negating and neutralizing the Ciceronian republic, transposes onto it the Christian believer's freedom. Only humility and love (charity) offer effective remedies to pagan superstition. But despite the idealization of that charity, it is also, within the context of a society, a political matter, a matter of politics.

In Spinoza's *Theological-Political Treatise*, the site of that devotion and that humility, in their social and political realities, will be contested and deciphered as the site of superstition. We are thus invited to move from one republic to another, from one city to another. Superstition, like all popular beliefs, misapprehends origins and the truth, in politics as well as in religion.[58] And the philosopher, somewhat like the theologian, finds himself obliged to produce a creed, no longer of grace, but of the freedom to philosophize.

2

Hobbes, or Nature as Reason

The Christian city sets in place a new *sociability*: its specificity, at least according to Augustine, lies in the truth of its social order, its recognition of a new kind of justice. In that city, natural law proceeds directly from divine law. It is, to be sure, an ideal or even utopian city, but one that, within the context of a historical critique, stands as the endpoint of a genesis of justice. Therefore, the bonds between the city and the "thing of the people" are characteristic of the authenticity and foundation of human institutions as a reflection of divine justice. Within that framework, any discussion of the city's law as constitutive of the social order must confront the problem of authority, or, more exactly, of the justification for authority. The Christian city, as an ideal, is authorized by a community of choice, by shared duties to the Creator. The actual city, governed by politics and human interests, seeks to find its justification in the reality of its institutions and their histories. It finds legitimacy in part by marking its distance from the ideal of the Christian city, by proclaiming its human character. That natural dimension of the polis is essential because it allows a shift toward a rational order, toward an emphasis on the role of reason in the formation of the city, its history, and its administration.

Imbecility

Hence in *On the Citizen* Thomas Hobbes recuperates (or, more precisely, strives to recuperate) the Christian dimension of the law in his definition of men's duties: "This book sets out men's duties, first as men, then as citizens, and lastly as Christians. These duties constitute the elements of the law of nature and of nations, the origin and force of justice and the essence of the Christian religion."[1]

For Hobbes, the individual is defined and characterized by the nature of his duties, by his relationship with nature and with other men, and by his relationship to God. He is therefore a *man* in the state of nature, a *citizen* in society, that is, in the human community, and a *Christian* in the universal community. That hierarchy or gradation explains the diversity of the law in terms of the means by which one belongs to a group. A man alone acts by might, a man in society by the force of law, the Christian by divine justice. Within that order, grace, the foundation of the Christian city, gives way to human reason: "[Law] is not in conflict with Divine right in that God gives commands to sovereigns through nature, i.e. through the dictates of natural reason."[2] Human law does not contradict divine law, by virtue of the nature of divine commandments and the means by which they are communicated. Nature is *reason* because it sets in place an order desired by the Creator; nature externalizes the divine message as a tangible, visible reality accessible to all. To justify that reason, to describe and explain it, Hobbes develops a hierarchy of divine communication. He sets in place a typology of divine speech that brings to mind many Augustinian passages devoted to the voice, the image, and the means of transmission of divine apparitions in the Old Testament.

Hobbes recognizes three forms of the word of God—internal speech, or *"the silent dictates of right reason"*; "direct revelation, which is . . . carried by a *supernatural voice,* or by a *vision";* and prophetic speech, which is expressed "through *the voice of a man . . .*

called a PROPHET." He believes it necessary to distinguish between God's natural speech, whatever it might be, and the way that human beings establish their laws.[3] That triad of divine communication stands opposed to the singleness of human communication. The material diversity of the means of divine communication contrasts with the poverty of human beings' communication. Human beings "promulgate their laws by *word* or *voice*; they have no other way of universally signifying their will."[4] The threefold structure of the word of God gives rise to an essential division that, according to Hobbes, characterizes the divine realm. On one hand is the natural order, the realm of common sense and reason; on the other, the prophetic order, which entails a choice, a selection, a privilege, and an election, which transcend reason. In accordance with that order, Hobbes describes two reigns of God or two covenants. The first reign, during which God ruled Adam and Eve, is characterized by the fact that God did not want to be shown "any obedience other than that which natural reason dictated."[5] That first covenant was broken and later replaced by a new covenant in which, according to Hobbes, God stipulated to Abraham "that I be your God and the God of your descendants after you for ever. And I will give to you and to your descendants after you the land of your wanderings."[6]

The shift from the first covenant to the second points to a dual recognition, an exchange and a reciprocity—and finally, a naturalization. That naturalization proceeds directly from the materiality of divine communication in the Old Testament. It reproduces the very nature of the act of communication in the second covenant, the one that followed the period of Adam and Eve (the first covenant). In his analysis of divine revelations, Hobbes, like Augustine before him, insists on the ambiguity of the texts and especially on the role played by the reception and interpretation of the divine message:

> No account is given of the form in which God appeared to *Abraham,* and what sound he made to address him, but it is

certain that *Abraham* believed that the voice was the voice of God and a true revelation, and that he wanted his followers to worship the one who had so addressed him as God, creator of the universe; and his faith lay not in believing that *God exists* or that his promises *are true* (which all men believe), but in not doubting that the one whose voice and promises he had heard was God. It is also clear that *God of Abraham* signifies not simply *God* but *God appearing to him,* just as the worship *Abraham* owed to God on that ground, was not the worship of *reason* but the worship of *religion* and *faith;* the worship which God, not reason, had revealed to him *by supernatural grace.*[7]

It is Abraham's faith that explains this divine communication. Furthermore, it is a communication derived from "supernatural grace," an election and a choice; it reflects the divine will to recognize and distinguish Abraham's fidelity and devotion. But that "supernatural grace" nevertheless remains inscribed in a subjective order, in an interpretation that ultimately reduces it to a special case, an exception marked by the context. For Hobbes, as a result, that supernatural grace does not translate into a transmission of the Law or a communication of laws desired by God. On the contrary, it is limited to an ambiguous generality: "We do not read of any laws given by God to *Abraham* or to his family, either then or later, either secular or sacred (with the exception of the one command about *circumcision,* which is in the *Agreement* itself). It is clear from this that there were no other laws or worship by which *Abraham* was bound, beyond the natural laws, rational worship and circumcision."[8]

The exception, that of an election transmitted by supernatural grace to Abraham and his family, does not go beyond the individual case. It does not formulate either a religion or laws. Hobbes extends and modifies that first contextualization and restriction of the nature and effects of the divine community in his description of prophecy, especially the prophecy of Moses. Regarding Moses, Hobbes seeks as well to naturalize, that is, to inscribe, revealed law in the order of natural reason, the functioning of the covenant, in order to eliminate the potential effects of election. In the case of Moses as in that of Abraham, it is the special individual character that in some sense determines the context and intelligibility of what the prophet offers the people, and also what he offers the historian in his interpretation: "Finally, we may infer that in *Moses's* lifetime the *interpretation of God's word* was not in the hands of any other Prophets whatever, from the fact we have already cited of his pre-eminence over all the others; and from natural reason, since the Prophet who carries the commands of God must also interpret them."[9]

Hobbes's insistence on the significance of the typology of God's word, its forms of materiality (its source, its transmission and reception, and so on), and on the interpretations these forms elicit, is intended to articulate the foundation of political power beyond any revelation and prophecy. In that context, the case of Moses is exemplary. Despite its specificity and supernatural character, it requires a political acknowledgment, an authorization that itself "authorizes" the political: "The authority then to admit books as God's Word lay with the king, and thus that book was approved and accepted by authority of King *Josiah*, as appears from 2 Kings 23.1–3, where we are told that he summoned the orders of the Kingdom, that is, the *Elders, Priests and Prophets* and *all the people,* and in their presence *he read the book* and *encouraged them to perform the words of this covenant,* i.e. he ensured that this Covenant was recognized as the *Covenant of Moses* i.e. as *God's Word,* and was once again accepted and confirmed by the *Israelites.*"[10]

The law of Moses comes into being through the law of acknowledgment by a political figure, and therefore the prophetic is subordinated to the political, and revelation to the law of natural reason. A political assembly renews the covenant and gives it all the luster of its authority. A monarch recognizes the law of the Monarch. Hobbes's evacuation of election as a whole, in favor of a naturalization of revelation within the structure of the law itself, has the objective, through the mutations of election and the maze of prophecy, of identifying the origins of the political, its structure and its history, independent of any direct divine intervention. Hobbes, moreover, seeks to define the church in terms of the nature and structure of divine speech, to view the church as an institution rooted in legality and subject to everything applicable to natural law. That desire to naturalize the authority of religion explains his insistence that Christ is not a lawmaker, that he proposes but does not establish laws.[11]

With Hobbes, it is the law of nature that bursts on the scene to explain the origin of the social order, its structure, and the manner of governing sociability. The justice he aims for is no longer that of Augustine: it is rather that of tolerance, that is, a justice that is primordially political because it acknowledges difference and diversity. And, somewhat like Augustine, Hobbes links the necessity of the law, of any law, to the very nature of man: "If God has the right to reign on the basis of his omnipotence, it is evident that men incur the *obligation* to obey him because of their imbecility."[12]

"Imbecility" is inscribed within a representation of humankind as an individual. But in Hobbes's case, childhood is no longer merely innocence or ignorance; rather, it represents a natural relationship to force and to law, a relationship that is at the heart of the law of nature: "Thus an evil man is rather like a sturdy boy, or a man of childish mind, and evil is simply want of reason at an age when it normally occurs to men by nature governed by discipline and experience of harm."[13]

The law, which is essentially political, cultivates and disciplines wickedness. It naturalizes the violent man; it civilizes him, in the sense that it transforms him into a member of society or of a city governed by laws.

3

Spinoza and the "Relics of Man's Ancient Bondage"

> The Psalmist addresses God, "Sacrifice and offering thou didst not desire, mine ears hast thou opened, burnt offering and sin-offering has thou not required, I delight to do thy will, o my God, yea, thy law is written in my inward parts." So it is only what is inscribed in the viscera, or soul, that the Psalmist calls God's law. [*Vocat igitur illam tantum legem Dei quae visceribus vel menti inscripta est*].
>
> *Benedictus de Spinoza*, Theological-Political Treatise, 60–61 [*translation modified*]

That detour through Hobbes was necessary to show the continued pertinence of the question of biblical election within the context of a reflection on the political and to identify one of the major reformulations, at the start of the modern era, of the Augustinian problematic. Hobbes proceeds to naturalize election and grace, in some sense by distinguishing and separating truth from revelation, by insisting on the human factors in the genesis of law and the political. Spinoza too will insist on the distinction between the law and truth. Like Augustine before him, he will privilege the heart, but a heart that, in occupying the space between the innate and the acquired, will be the organ of philosophy and not that of the truth of a religion or of religion in general; it will be the agent of freedom and no longer that of authority and obedience. For Spinoza the heart—and even the viscera—is the soul where the true nature of God resides and where that nature is revealed to man, to every man. And the heart is a place of inscription, a writing surface that receives divine law. But the Spinozan heart is not the same as the Augustinian heart: it is not the place of a mystical encounter with the Creator. The two choices Spinoza makes will define a good part of the philosophical legacy—at least in the seventeenth and eighteenth centuries, especially in Germany—in debates surrounding revelation and religion.

The Republic and the "Relics of Man's Ancient Bondage"

For Spinoza, election in the classical sense of the term is impossible on principle, because it would rest on a nature and a conception of the spirit and of God different from his own. Despite that impossibility, the *Theological-Political Treatise* and the *Ethics* reflect once more on the conditions of possibility for biblical election, for its misapprehension, and for its transformations. In addition, Spinoza's argument follows a path similar to that of Augustine: it calls into question the truth of the revelations of the divine in the Old Testament, of prophecy and of its status; it elaborates a typology of the divine word, of its manifestations and their meanings, reception, and interpretations; and it generates a dual creed, that of religion and theology and that of philosophy. Spinoza inscribes his discourse within a general critique of superstition and its impact on human understanding. But instead of limiting himself, as Augustine does, to the superstitions of pagans, he broadens and deepens the field of superstition's applicability until it incorporates a large part of all religious beliefs, including those derived from the Bible. Furthermore, the genesis of superstition, like that of election for Augustine, is directly linked to a misreading, a founding misapprehension of the nature of the divine message.

From the start, then, at the very heart of Spinoza's undertaking is the critique of superstition. Augustine defines superstition in terms of its association with pagan practices linked to idol worship, but for Spinoza, superstition originates in a significant displacement emblematic of its genesis and its authority. Superstition, in its appeal to the supernatural and its fictions, constitutes a turning to the lower realms, to the animalistic. Hence superstition, born of fear and the desire for "fortune's favors," in abandoning reason and enlightenment, valorizes what for Spinoza symbolizes an absolute misapprehension:

> This being the case, we see that it is particularly those who greedily covet fortune's favors who are the readiest victims of superstition of every kind, and it is especially when they are helpless in danger that they implore God's help with prayers and womanish tears. Reason they call blind, . . . and human wisdom they call vain, while the delusions of the imagination, dreams, and other childish absurdities are taken to be the oracles of God. Indeed, they think that God, spurning the wise, has written his decrees not in man's mind but in the entrails of beasts, or that by divine inspiration and instigation these decrees are foretold by fools, madmen or birds. To such madness are men driven by their fears [*Tantum timor homines insanire facit*].[1]

The animalistic replaces the human, just as fantasy and madness take the place of reason. Superstition is a perversion of reality and of the nature of things—a perversion that has the power to drive men mad and to make them believe. It institutes fear as the origin of law, of any law, whether divine or human, social or political. Hence, the aim of Spinoza's analysis is to demonstrate the falseness of superstition's origin and of its effects, thereby calling into question everything it institutes and everything it has instituted. Fear occupies the site of a profound misapprehension: an ignorance of man, of nature, and of the order of the world. Superstition, as protection against fear, can explain political misdeeds and religious prejudices. To examine superstition critically, one must clarify the nature of religion and of religious superstition and also account for the political model it authorizes. "For this purpose my most urgent task has been to indicate the main prejudices that prevail regarding religion—that is, the relics of man's ancient bondage—and then again the prejudices regarding the right of civil authorities."[2]

Spinoza is explicating the title of his book word for word: the theological and the political are inextricably intertwined, inasmuch as, in popular prejudices, both stem from superstition and superstitious beliefs. In addition, throughout its history superstition has transferred to the political what originally belonged only to the religious. That extension, that prolongation of the initial perversion explains "the supreme mystery of despotism, its prop and stay, [which] is to keep men in a state of deception, and with the specious title of religion to cloak the fear by which they must be held in check, so that they will fight for their servitude as if for salvation."[3]

As in Augustine, but from a completely different viewpoint, the republic, the "thing of the people," necessarily invokes the political and the religious; it proves to be the place of the true city's genesis. From the first steps in the theological-political argument, the radicality of Spinoza's approach becomes clearer, first, by virtue of its generality and second, by its insistence on the centrality of the political dimension of superstition and, as a corollary, of the historicity of institutions and beliefs. Hence the philosophical critique of superstition has to be a philological and historical study, as well as a conceptual one. It is within this context that the notion of election will be considered, as an exemplary case illustrating the misapprehensions and errors produced by the perverse effects of ignorance about the nature of God.

Before continuing our examination of the Old Testament, let us recall the appendix to part 1 of the *Ethics*, in which Spinoza formulates the genesis of superstition, describing the formation and transformation of prejudice into superstition.

> It will suffice here for me to take as a basis of argument what must be admitted by all: that is, that all men are born ignorant of the causes of things [*quod omnes homines rerum causarum ignari nascuntur*], and that all have a desire of seeking what is useful to them; that they are conscious, moreover, of this. From these premises it follows then, that men think themselves free [*se liberose esse*] inasmuch as they are conscious of their volitions and appetites, and as they are ignorant of the causes by which they are led to seek and to will, they do not even dream of [the] existence [of these causes]. It follows, in the second place, that men do all things with an end in view, that is, they seek what is useful. . . . Furthermore, as they find in themselves and without themselves many things which aid them not a little in the quest of things useful to themselves . . . they consider all natural things to be means towards what is useful to them; and as they know that they found these means as they were, and did not make them themselves, herein they have cause for believing that some one else prepared these means for their use. . . . But they must conclude from the means which they are wont to prepare for themselves, that there is some governor or governors [of nature] [*naturae rectores*], endowed with human freedom, who have taken care of all things for them and have made all things for their use. They must form an estimate of the nature of these governors from their own. . . : and hence they come to say that the Gods direct all things for the use of men, that men may be bound to them and do them the highest honour. Whence it has come about that each individual has devised, in accordance with his own nature, different ways of worshipping God, that God may love him above the rest and direct the whole of nature for the gratification of his blind cupidity and insatiable avarice.

Thus this prejudice became a superstition [*Atque ita hoc praejudicium in superstitionem versum*], and fixed its roots deeply in the mind, and this was the reason why all diligently endeavoured to understand and explain the final causes of all things.[4]

Original ignorance explains the prejudice at the origin of superstition. The human being, misapprehending himself, also misapprehends the nature of God. He constructs God in his own image and imagines him as if God were another self, more powerful, of course, but nevertheless a being like himself, endowed with freedom, and, above all, with desires. God thereby is essentially not a creator but a protector. He is, according to Spinoza, a rector, that is, someone who directs. Man's egoism, the foremost sign of his ignorance, is the source of anthropomorphism. Furthermore, that egoism casts and designates God himself in egotistical terms. Man, creator of false gods (or, to borrow Spinoza's formulation, of the gods), erects a deity who is in quest of recognition and reciprocity, a quest that would explain religious cults and traditions, the superstitions of humankind. In this case, the multiplicity of religions lies in the diversity of the human being, a diversity that reflects the variety and creative power of human greed, human will, human appetite. Religions exist because men exist and do not know themselves. That diversity explains not only the existence of different religions but also the existence of schisms within a single religion. Superstition thus stands at the origin of human religion; it accounts for its genesis and for its evolution. In the last instance, it provides access to the human foundations of religious beliefs.

Election and Circumcision

In chapter 3 of the *Theological-Political Treatise*, Spinoza expounds his ideas on the Jewish people's election in the Old Testament. The title of the chapter ("Of the Vocation of the Hebrews, and Whether the

Gift of Prophecy Was Peculiar to Them") in itself suggests Spinoza's views on the question. His argument, like Augustine's, proceeds by insisting on the specificity of what is recounted in scripture, on the context and, above all, on the import, scope, and true significance of the text: "However, although we assert that Moses was speaking to the understanding of the Hebrews in the passages of the Pentateuch just quoted, we do not mean to deny that God ordained those laws in the Pentateuch for them alone, nor that he spoke only to them, nor that the Hebrews witnessed marvels such have never befallen any other nation. Our point is merely this, that Moses wished to admonish the Hebrews in a particular way, using such reasoning as would bind them more firmly in the worship of God, having regard to the immaturity of their understanding."[5]

For Spinoza, what is particularly striking about the texts under discussion is their language and the way that choice of language reflects the Hebrews' state. (That "childish mind" or "immaturity of understanding" of the chosen people will prove propitious in later philosophers' efforts to articulate the need to move beyond election as a notion constitutive of the religious specificity of the Old Testament.) Moses fashions his discourse as a function of his audience. Hence, from the start, the universality of election, its absolute truth, is reduced to a local question. "Further, we wished to show that the Hebrews surpassed other nations not in knowledge nor in piety, but in quite a different respect; or (to adopt the language of Scripture directed to their understanding) that the Hebrews were chosen by God above all others not for the true life nor for any higher understanding—though often admonished thereto—but for a quite different purpose."[6] The localization of election leads to its diversification.

That particularization of election is based on two factors: first, the absence of direct communication between God and the Jewish people (all the prophecies required signs and mediations, which are sources of confusion and misapprehension); and second, a generalization of the notion of election—through the idea of God's "external help"—to the choice of a mode of life.[7] Election is a form and a way of life chosen by God for each individual; it consists of the choice of place, form of government, and laws, and is unrelated to salvation. In other words, it is naturalized and detached from anything supernatural. It is therefore clear why Spinoza radically rejects the very notion of election in the broad sense of the term. For him, election is the symptom of the power of superstition, and especially of the misapprehension of God's true law. Is it necessary to point out that there is no grace in Spinoza's philosophy? The Jewish people's election is a limited election; it concerns only the form and duration of the government and the nature of its laws: "Through this alone, then, do nations differ from one another, namely, in respect of the kind of society and laws under which they live and are governed. Thus the Hebrew nation was chosen by God before all others not by reason of its understanding nor of its spiritual qualities, but by reason of its social organisation and the good fortune whereby it achieved supremacy and retained it for so many years."[8]

Spinoza insists on that uniqueness of the Jewish people's election and explains: "For as God chose them only for the establishing of a special kind of society and state, they must also have had laws of a special kind."[9] And he adds: "A merely casual perusal clearly reveals that the Hebrews surpassed other nations in this alone, that they were successful in achieving security for themselves and overcame great dangers, and this chiefly by God's external help alone. In other respects they were no different from other nations, and God was equally gracious to all."[10] What is special here is the law given to the chosen people. That law is no longer a sign of their unique relationship with God, but rather represents the specificity of election and distinguishes their society from the rest of humanity. Spinoza thereby devalorizes the absolute aspect of election by reintroducing it into a context where God speaks and communicates to all nations in his own way. It is true that his communication with the Hebrew people is special, marked by prophecy: "As to whether God ordained special laws for other nations as well and revealed himself through prophecy for their lawgivers—that is, under those attributes by which they were accustomed to imagine God—I cannot be sure. But this at least is evident from Scripture, that other nations also had their own state and their special laws by God's external guidance."[11]

Prophecy, it seems, is a specialty of the Jewish people. God communicates in a different way with other nations, offering them laws appropriate to them. Election is a general economy with diverse local manifestations. It is one of the forms in which peoples imagine their relation to their creator. And the law prescribed by election can only be a law addressing a people in a particular place and time. In other words, election is not the exclusive revelation of the Law: it is only *a* revelation of *a* law.

But the specificity of Jewish election is not limited to prophecy alone. For Spinoza, the interpreter of Paul, prophecy signifies a specific form of writing associated with the Jewish people and the modality of its election: "So when [Paul] says, 'To the Jews alone were entrusted the oracles of God,' we should either take it as meaning that only to the Jews were the laws entrusted in writing while to other nations they were communicated by revelation and conception alone, or we must say (since Paul's aim is to refute objections that could be raised only by the Jews) that Paul is answering in accordance with the understanding and beliefs of the Jews of that time."[12] Prophecy is also distinguished by its external signs, and especially by circumcision. Spinoza explains the temporal and local nature of Jewish election by insisting on the isolation of the Jewish state and by casting into relief the determining role of ritual practices. Hence the famous passage on circumcision:

> [The Jews] have separated themselves from other nations to such a degree as to incur the hatred of all, and this not only through external rites alien to the rites of other nations but also through the mark of circumcision, which they most religiously

observe. That they are preserved largely through the hatred of other nations is demonstrated by historical fact. . . . Indeed, were it not that the fundamental principles of their religion discourage manliness, I would not hesitate to believe that they will one day, given the opportunity—such is the mutability of human affairs—establish once more their independent state, and that God will again choose them.[13]

Election, being temporal, can recur. Although the Jewish people distinguishes itself from others by inward and outward signs, it is nonetheless true—and despite the power of that choice—that the Jewish case is not unique. Spinoza offers his reader a comparison drawn from the history of another nation: China. He naturalizes circumcision by introducing it into a comparative economy, by assimilating it to one gesture among other possible gestures:

> The Chinese afford us an outstanding example. . . . They, too, religiously observe the custom of the pigtail which sets them apart from all other people, and they have preserved themselves as a separate people for so many thousands of years that they far surpass all other nations in antiquity. . . . In conclusion, should anyone be disposed to argue that the Jews, for this reason or any other, have been chosen by God unto eternity, I shall not oppose him, provided that he holds that this election, be it temporal or eternal, in so far as it is peculiar to the Jews, is concerned only with the nature of their commonwealth and their material welfare . . . whereas in respect of understanding and true virtue there is no distinction between one nation and another.[14]

It appears that, for Spinoza, the corporeal marks of election do not suffice to transform it into a unique or universal election. The true God does not choose between nations or peoples: he simply speaks to nations in languages they understand.

The Pick of Mankind

To better appreciate the radicality of Spinoza's positions, we have only to compare them to those in Judah Halevi's *Kuzari* (Judah was born in Spain ca. 1075).[15] The *Kuzari* is a digest of the orthodox interpretation of election and its unique status, and a celebrated classic defending the Jewish religion. Furthermore, given the very logic of its argument against the two other monotheistic religions, it accentuates and crystallizes the specificity of the Jewish people's "vocation," to borrow Spinoza's expression from the *Theological-Political Treatise*.

The *Kuzari* elaborates a detailed defense of the covenant and of election, a defense rooted in the absolute privileges of an absolute and unparalleled divine choice. For Judah, then, everything, from the language of the chosen people to the rites of the law, is a sign of the founding gesture and moment of the chosen people's history and destiny. From that perspective, it is tempting to read Spinoza's *Theological-Political Treatise* as a refutation, or more accurately, as a philosophical correction of the *Kuzari*, especially since Judah defends the "despised religion"[16] not only against Christianity and Islam but also and especially against the harmful influences of philosophy (Muslim philosophy pervaded by Greek knowledge) on the reception and interpretation of religion, particularly that of the chosen people.

From the viewpoint of the *Kuzari*, election is decisive: it inaugurates the true history of the people of God and constitutes the community chosen by the Creator. In addition, it introduces an insurmountable difference between the chosen people and the rest of humankind, a difference that is irreducible and irreversible:

> *Al Khazari:* If this be so, then your belief is a legacy [*waqf*] confined to yourselves?
> *The Rabbi:* Yes; but any Gentile who joins us unconditionally shares our good fortune, without, however, being quite

equal to us. If the Law were binding on us only because God created us, the white and the black man would be equal, since He created them all. But the Law was given to us because He led us out of Egypt, and remained attached to us, because we are the pick of mankind.[17]

In the original Arabic, election is a *waqf,* an inalienable legacy, but also a gift that must be maintained and protected, a gift that requires a particular devotion. Being the "pick of mankind," the world's elite, grants one a status outside the norm, a situation without equal, which stems from an unparalleled divine choice. And that divine choice finds expression in an attachment that explains both the specificity of the Jewish people's history and its traditions, its language. That dimension of election, that distinction, explains in great part the insistence of the *Kuzari* on the incomparable aspect or dimension of the Jewish people's history. Judah develops an argument that is at once a summation of what election is from the orthodox point of view and, at the same time, a refutation of the corruption or perversion by philosophical discourse of the monotheistic religion or religions. The defense of the "despised religion" is thus an exposition of what election truly is, of its effects in history, and of how it forms and fashions the unfolding of history. It is also an argument against comparison, against any comparison between those who are chosen and the rest of humankind, even those who, in their way, recognize a share of truth in the covenant. The chosen one is apart; above all, he is alone. He is incomparable. Even conversion would not suffice to transmit certain privileges of election:

> *The Rabbi:* . . . Now we do not allow any one who embraces our religion theoretically by means of a word alone to take equal rank with ourselves, but demand actual self-sacrifice, purity, knowledge, circumcision, and numerous religious ceremonies. The convert must adopt our mode of life entirely. We must bear

in mind that the rite of circumcision is a divine mark made by God in the member of the ruling passion, so that it should be curbed. . . . Those, however, who become Jews do not take equal rank with born Israelites, who are specially privileged to attain to prophecy, whilst the former can only achieve something by learning from them, and can only become pious and learned, but never prophets.[18]

Conversion, associated with the practice of rites, has its limits. It cannot give access to what, for Judah, constitutes the inevitable companion of election, namely, prophecy. Herein lies the radicality of the *Kuzari*'s position, its insistence on a genealogical link associated with the very notion of election as legacy, or *waqf*. It is in this precise sense that the Jewish people is the "pick of mankind." Its election is both the mark and the gift of speech and language, a gift of prophetic speech that marks history and establishes the pattern of its unfolding. That election bears its historical marks: circumcision and prophecy. Whereas Spinoza contextualizes and relativizes circumcision by comparing it to the queues of the ancient Chinese, the *Kuzari* assigns it a function that transcends place and local beliefs by linking it directly to the Creator's will to mark his desire on the body of his chosen people. The *Kuzari* expounds an absolutism of the unique and the distinct; by contrast, Spinoza retraces everywhere in religious history the relativism of local diversity. These two models of election are two different ways of putting in play what in the Old Testament text constitutes the driving force of relations between God and his people, an actualization conveyed by speech, by place, and above all by the materiality of the history following from election and shaping the most visible sign of revelation. Therefore, the *Kuzari*'s insistence that the practices of election, its rites and traditions, are inseparable from the very identity of the community accentuates the founding dimension of election. It casts into relief the continuity between divine, individual, and collective choice. Election *makes* a community and a nation: it forms a unique body, a notion that is diametrically opposed to that of the church as a mystical body or the *Ummah* as the nation of the last prophecy.

Election literalizes divine choice by inscribing it on the body and in the voice of the chosen people. In one case, election is a restricted body, while in the other, in the *Ecclesia* or the *Ummah*, it is an ever-expanding body. Election thus seems to found diverse models of the social, corresponding to very different conceptions of the collective body: as a body both physical and "subtle," it becomes the site of a dispute over how God chooses to reveal himself and over the historical consequences or repercussions of that determining choice. For Judah, election gives rise to a single nation, a chosen nation. And that nation, according to the *Kuzari*, has its language and its territory: "Priority belongs, in the first instance, to the people which, as stated before, is the essence and kernel [of the nations]. In the second instance, it would belong to [the country], on account of the religious acts connected with it, which I would compare to the cultivation of the vineyard."[19]

That priority is also what explains the transmission of election, by means of language and speech, from an individual to a series of individuals and, in the end, to an entire people:

The Rabbi: . . . There were some, however, among them who did not come under divine influence, as Terah, but his son Abraham was the disciple of his grandfather Eber, and was born in the lifetime of Noah. Thus the divine spirit descended from the grandfather to the grandchildren. Abraham represented the chosen one among the children of Eber, being his disciple, and for this reason he was called *Ibri*. Eber represented the chosen one among the descendants of Shem, and Shem the chosen one among those of Noah. He inherited the temperate zone, the centre and principal part of which is Palestine, the land of prophecy. Japheth turned towards north, and Ham towards south. . . . The sons of [Jacob] were all chosen, all worthy of the divine influence, as well as of the country distinguished by the divine spirit. This is the first instance of the divine influence descending on a number of people, whereas it had previously only been vouchsafed to isolated individuals. Then God tended them in Egypt, multiplied and aggrandised them, as a tree with a sound root grows until it produces perfect fruit, resembling the first fruit from which it was planted, viz. Abraham, Isaac, Jacob, Joseph and his brethren. The seed further produced Moses.[20]

But that economy of election and of its transmission also governs the language of prophecy. And it explains the unique status of the Hebrew language in the history of the divine choice:

The Rabbi: [Hebrew] shared the fate of its bearers, degenerating and dwindling with them. Considered historically and logically, however, it is by its very essence the noblest language. According to tradition, it is the language in which God spoke to Adam and Eve, and in which the latter conversed. It is proved by the derivation of Adam from *adāmāh* [earth], *ishshāh* [woman] from *ish* [man]; *ḥayyāh* [Eve] from *ḥayy* [living]. . . . It is the language of Eber after whom it was called *Hebrew*, because after the confusion of tongues it was he who retained it. . . . The superiority of Hebrew is manifest from the logical point of view if we consider the people who employed it for discourses, particularly at the time when prophecy was rife among them, also for preaching, songs, and psalmody.[21]

The fate of the divine language is linked to the fate of the people that uses it: the history of one and of the other is a play of echoes and of mirrors that reflect a twofold justification for the superiority of the language of election: first, a historical justification through the temporality of history itself (which will be found again in Blaise

Pascal's *Pensées*); and second, a more "philosophical" explanation, based on the intimate connection between language and prophecy. In the argument of the *Kuzari*, everything can be explained by a dual choice: that of God and that of the chosen people. History does nothing more than attest to the truth of that covenant and that exchange. In addition, for Judah, election translates into a privilege unique in the history of religion, that of the bond between the people of Israel and the divine: "*Adonāi* is, therefore, called rightly the God of Israel, because this view [of God] is not found among Gentiles."[22]

Errors and Mediation

Through language, we once more encounter the essential problem raised by Spinoza concerning election—that of its nature, its structure, and especially its scope. Is it, as Spinoza believes, a temporal and local election marked by the necessities of the historical place and circumstances, or rather, as the *Kuzari* has it, an election without equal that can take place only once? Is it a restricted election that can have historical variations, or a universal and unlimited election? Whereas the *Kuzari* explains the shift from the election of an individual to that of a people and a nation by means of divine will, Spinoza uncovers the mechanisms of this shift from limited election to a generalized election. To illustrate the genesis of this confusion and this error in reading and interpretation, we have only to recall Spinoza's explanation for Adam's disobedience in the Genesis narrative:

> So if, for example, God said to Adam that he willed that Adam should not eat of the tree of knowledge of good and evil, it would have been a contradiction in terms for Adam to be able to eat of that tree. And so it would have been impossible for Adam to eat of it, because that divine decree must have involved eternal necessity and truth. However, since Scripture tells us that God did so command Adam, and that Adam did nevertheless

eat of the tree, it must be accepted that God revealed to Adam only the punishment he must incur if he should eat of that tree; the necessary entailment of that punishment was not revealed. Consequently, Adam perceived this revelation not as an eternal and necessary truth but as a law, that is to say, an enactment from which good or ill consequence would ensue not from the intrinsic nature of deed performed but only from the will and absolute power of some ruler. . . . If God had spoken to them directly, employing no physical means, they would have perceived this not as a law but as an eternal truth.[23]

Spinoza discusses this first conversation between God and man several times in the *Theological-Political Treatise*. Hence, "Adam, to whom God was first revealed, did not know that God is omnipotent and omniscient, for he hid from God and attempted to excuse his sin before God as if he had to do with a man. So in his case, too, God was revealed in accordance with his understanding."[24] Adam imagines God as a man, in his own image, and therefore God reveals himself to Adam solely in keeping with Adam's faculties and capacities. Later, Spinoza seems to concede another interpretation of the creation narrative, an interpretation that views the first divine commandment as the condensation of "natural Divine Law" and the "natural light of reason." And, he adds, "it would not be difficult to explain on this basis the whole narrative or parable of the first man, but I refrain from doing so for two reasons. First, I cannot be absolutely sure that my explanation would be in agreement with the author's intention; secondly, there are many who do not grant that this narrative is a parable, firmly maintaining that it is a straightforward account of fact."[25]

The way God communicates with man determines the nature of the interpretation of his speech and sets in motion the development of laws. Furthermore, the first couple's misapprehension inaugurates the confusion between the law chosen for one place and one people and eternal truths. That primordial ignorance stems in some sense from the need for mediation, for representations of the divine message through figures, voices, and visions. Within that context, election, which is in reality the appropriate choice for everyone, is transformed into a privilege and a privileged relation to God, and in that sense results from superstition, since it translates primitive fear into order. Yet divine, universal, and natural law does not need historical narratives, "whatever their content," which are the source of prejudices and superstitions. Spinoza directly links misinterpretation to mediation; he portrays the origin of human and social laws as the product of mediated communication. In view of that, it hardly matters what language was spoken by Adam and Eve or even by God in his communications with them. It is the very choice to speak through a language that introduces error into the history of humankind. Furthermore, Spinoza's critical examination of election neutralizes, so to speak, all the effects of election detailed in the *Kuzari*. His analysis seems to coincide with Augustine's in that it links mediation to error, or in that it connects, within the history of revelation, immediacy and internal communication to authenticity, or better, to universality. For Spinoza, there is a universal principle resulting from the absence of direct revelation, and that principle explains even the relation to the image within Judaism:

> Nor did the Law revealed to Moses—to which nothing might be added and from which nothing might be taken away, and which was established as the nation's statutes—ever require us to believe that God is incorporeal or that he has no form or figure, but only that he is God, in whom the Jews must believe and whom alone they must worship. And to dissuade them from forsaking his worship, it forbade them to assign an image to him or to make any; for as they had not seen God's image, any image they could make would not resemble God but must necessarily resemble some created thing which they had seen.[26]

A face-to-face relationship and direct communication seem to be the sign of a general authenticity and truth, without boundaries or limits. In fact, "we may quite clearly understand that God can communicate with man without mediation, for he communicates his essence to our minds without employing corporeal means. Nevertheless, a man who can perceive by pure intuition that which is not contained in the basic principles of our cognition and cannot be deduced therefrom must needs possess a mind whose excellence far surpasses the human mind."[27] The privilege of a communication without the mediation of the body requires, quite simply, a superior nature.

Here Spinoza seems to be privileging the figure of Christ as the only figure to have communicated directly with God, without intermediaries: "Therefore I do not believe that anyone has attained such a degree of perfection surpassing all others, except Christ. To him God's ordinances leading men to salvation were revealed not by words or by visions, but directly. . . . The Voice of Christ can thus be called the Voice of God in the same way as that which Moses heard."[28]

It is by virtue of that communication that Christ is not the author of new laws but rather the messenger of universal ethics:

> With regard to Christ, although he also appears to have laid down laws in God's name, we must maintain that he perceived things truly and adequately; for Christ was not so much a prophet as the mouthpiece of God. . . . And surely . . . God revealed himself to Christ, or to Christ's mind, directly, and not through words and images as in the case of the prophets. . . . For Christ, as I have said, was not sent to preserve the state and to institute laws, but only to teach the universal law.
>
> Hence we can readily understand that Christ by no means abrogated the law of Moses, for it was not Christ's purpose to introduce new laws into the commonwealth. His chief concern was to teach moral doctrines, keeping them distinct from the laws of the commonwealth.[29]

Despite the unique status of Christ, Spinoza does not privilege Christianity. Far from it. He contests its legitimacy as the narrative fulfillment of the Old Testament and everything that follows from it. Furthermore, he seems to separate Christ from the history of religions, since he considers him a manifestation of universal law. For Spinoza, Christ is a figure outside religions. That evacuation of Christianity stems from the same logic Spinoza used to localize the election of the Jewish people, and installs a radical separation between religions as political institutions and universal ethics. In its way, Spinoza's Christ anticipates Nietzsche's in the *Antichrist*. And, as later for Nietzsche, the characterization of Christ is for Spinoza only the preamble to a critique of Christianity, its history and institutions, and also its relation to Judaism.

It is within the context of defining and discussing faith that Spinoza exploits the distinction between Christ and Christianity, between Christ and the church, by insisting on the cleavage introduced into faith by obedience. Hence faith no longer has any autonomy or power: it derives its authority from the obedience it requires. Furthermore, the salvation it promises is only the result of that obedience and, Spinoza says, "it follows that faith requires not so much true dogmas as pious dogmas, that is, such as move the heart to obedience."[30] Like election, faith is pervaded by its institutional context, which, from its origin, detaches it from the true nature of God. And the section of the *Theological-Political Treatise* devoted to religion and faith concludes with the invention of a creed in two parts: the first creed is that of the churches that have gone astray, and it details the human and historical genesis and institution of both faith and its dogmas; the second, by contrast, "allows to every man the utmost freedom to philosophise."[31] Philosophy, dedicated to freedom, is also open to other institutional forms, to a different city, to the city inspired by philosophy and the freedom it procures.

Augustine contests election in order to recuperate it in the Incarnation through grace; Spinoza inserts election into a historical and political context, generalizing and naturalizing it with the aim of legitimating the freedom to philosophize. From one to the other—and from one symbol to another—we witness parallel approaches, similar methods that portray the determining connections between revelation and its manifestations. But these parallel approaches culminate in opposing results. For Augustine, the unique status of election is recuperated within the economy of grace. For Spinoza, by contrast, election is diversified because it is universal; it is shared because it concerns only laws and human affairs. Two different conceptions of superstition give rise to two different models of the city: on one hand, a battle for the preeminence of Christian theology and its absolute legitimacy; on the other, a plea in defense of an enlightened republic founded on tolerance and philosophical conversation. Between the two paths, processes take shape that appear at first sight to converge, especially in how they approach and deal with the legacy of the Old Testament; in reality, however, they stand radically opposed. Spinoza does not hesitate to formulate the creed of faith or theology, a creed that is a universal dogma. Hence Spinoza reduces the critical examination of scripture, election, and prophecy, as well as of the texts of the New Testament, to a twofold principle or proposition: first, a belief, namely, that there is a "Supreme Being who loves justice and charity"; and second, a fact, that "faith demands piety rather than truth; faith is pious and saving only by reason of the obedience it inspires."[32] It seems that any discussion of election must lead to a discussion of the city and of the political. But before briefly expounding the Spinozan version of the "thing of the people," let us consider a few of Pascal's fragments devoted to election and to the history it makes possible. In the ideas expressed in these fragments, Pascal is a "solitary traveler."

The Pascalian Exception, or, The Visibility of Election

Where Spinoza insists on the reality and specificity of Jewish election in order to place it within a restricted context, Pascal develops an entirely different argument in favor of the universal truth and authenticity of the chosen people's history. Pascal's approach may be considered surprising, especially since it aspires to be comparative.

How to decide among all the world's religions? How to choose among the different religious narratives available? What criteria of truth can guide someone pondering the authenticity of religious histories? To respond to these questions, Pascal undertakes a comparison among the great nations known to us: he chooses to place together, to compare, the texts and narratives of pagans (that is, the Egyptians, the Greeks, and the Romans), those of China, and of course, the texts of the Old Testament. For him, everything plays out in a dual register: first, in the very nature of the texts and narratives in question; and second, in the relation between the texts and their authors. This means that Pascal appears to set in place a system of comparison and evaluation that takes into account the materiality of the object (with everything that choice entails); the nature of the text (poem, fable, romance, history, and so on); and finally, the links between the author or authors of the texts and the historical object. That Pascalian method offers an alternative to Spinoza's critical and historical analysis (and even to that adopted by Augustine in his examination of the Old Testament texts). And Pascal articulates the foundations of his "method" in the clearest terms possible: it is founded in the act of bearing witness. "*Falseness of other religions.* They have no witnesses; these people have. God challenges other religions to produce such signs: Is. XLIII. 9–XLIV. 8."[33] The distinctive mark of the chosen people is the act of witnessing, a unique act for Pascal.

Pagan histories such as that of China are mythical and deficient in historical truth because they are not produced by true witnesses, by contemporaries. According to the Pascalian logic regarding the veracity of historical narratives, the historian or storyteller must necessarily be present, that is, he is first and foremost a witness to what he describes. Furthermore, Pascal's positing of that necessary condition is only the first step toward a more radical position: that of identifying the text with the people, the book with a community's fate. Pascal insists on that identification between a people and its book as the absolute mark of the truth of its religion:

> *Antiquity of the Jews.* What a difference there is between one book and another! I am not surprised that the Greeks composed the *Iliad*, nor the Egyptians and Chinese their histories. You have only to see how that came about. These historians of fable were not contemporary with the things they wrote about. Homer composed a tale, offered and accepted as such. . . .
> Any history that is not contemporary is suspect: thus the Sibylline books and those of Trismegistus, and many others which have enjoyed credit in the world, are false and have been found to be false in the course of time. This is not the case with contemporary authors.
> There is a great difference between a book composed by an individual, which he hands over to the people, and a book that a people composes itself. It is beyond doubt that the book is as old as the people.[34]

That identification of a people with a text is crucial because, at least for Pascal, it allows one to distinguish and separate the accounts he claims are true from historical fables and tales. That Pascalian valorization of the chosen people's act of witnessing is all the more striking if we recall his arguments in the *Pensées* regarding the comparison—which would subsequently become classic for all Christian authors—between the synagogue and the church. There he describes and explains the relationship between Judaism and Christianity: "The Synagogue did not perish, because it was figurative. But because it was only figurative it fell into slavery. The figure continued to exist until the coming of the truth so that the Church should always be visible either in the image which promised it or in the actual effect."[35] For Pascal, Judaism, despite its "literalism," constitutes the conjoined twin of Christianity: their histories are intimately connected by their acts of witnessing.

Contemporary acts of witnessing, accompanied by fidelity to the text, open the way to another approach to the question of the local and the universal, the temporal and the eternal. In formulating as an essential criterion of truth the authenticity and historicity specific to the founding texts of religion, Pascal surreptitiously valorizes Hebrew election. He defends it not only by showing its reality but also by demonstrating its effects in and on history. It is at that level that his analysis may be seen to coincide with Spinoza's, especially if we take into account the essential role that Spinoza assigns to sincerity. In this respect, it would be necessary to measure all the differences, as well as the possible similarities, between historical sincerity and Pascalian witnessing.

The Jewish people's temporal and local election gives rise to a special society and the laws proper to it. Election, in this case, explains and describes the genesis of the social and political in a determined context. It is in this precise sense that election marks the collective body, just as it marks the individual body. According to Pascal, these markings of the two bodies constitute the proof of election. The "corporeal" and visible marks are for him the marks of truth: "I see then makers of religions in several parts of the world and throughout the ages, but their morality fails to satisfy me and their proofs fail to give me pause. Thus I should have refused alike the Moslem religion, that of China, of the ancient Romans, and of the Egyptians solely because, none of them bearing the stamp of truth more than another, nor anything which forces me to choose it, reason cannot incline towards one rather than another."[36] Truth is signed by blood and sacrifice, by devotion and the obstinate defense of revealed truth: "*History of China.* I only believe histories whose witnesses are ready to be put to death."[37]

The identification of the chosen people with the book that shaped it, as Pascal often repeats, leads him to modify his conception of prophecy, or, more precisely, to define it in a way that makes it compatible with his idea of historical and biblical witnessing. External signs must no longer be sought to prove prophecies. On the contrary, "to prophesy is to speak of God, not by outward proofs, but from an inward immediate feeling."[38] Here prophecy coincides with immediacy, a view that sets aside all the difficulties raised by Augustine and Spinoza in their respective examinations of divine manifestation in the Old Testament. For them, prophecy is only a bearing witness, inward to be sure, and one that can find expression in public speech, but first and foremost a bearing witness. It is only the figure, in the Pascalian sense of the term, for the act of bearing witness to the origins of a book and a people—another sign of continuity—and especially for the formative power of election. The book makes prophecy visible, just as bearing witness makes election visible. For Pascal, that visibility is one of the truths of Christianity because it provides proof of that religion through the history of the chosen people: "Carnal Jews are midway between Christians and heathen. The heathen do not know God and love only earthly things, the Jews know the true God and love only earthly things, Christians know the true God and do not love earthly things. Jews and heathen love the same goods; Jews and Christians know the same God. The Jews were of two kinds: some only had heathen, others had Christian impulses."[39]

Although Pascal privileges bearing witness in his defense of biblical religion, he also links the political structure to the form of the community's founding text, thereby maintaining a historical coherence for Christianity and its politics. Spinoza, by contrast, identifies the principal objective of his book as being to distinguish between theology and philosophy, with the aim of separating the contemporary and modern political from any authoritarian model. In that sense, he replicates Augustine's choice, a method that inspired Pascal's elaboration of election and its intimate connections to the historical truth of religion. Spinoza offers his reader a dual creed: the first theological, the second philosophical. To a great extent, he adopts the "thing of the people" with its Ciceronian roots against the Augustinian interpretation of the pagan city. The freedom to philosophize stands opposed to theological pedagogy. It sets in place another pedagogy, that of the new citizen who has "freedom of thought, and of saying what one thinks."[40]

Citizen's Freedom

Augustine founded the legitimacy of the city on grace, the motivating force of human politics, the agent of justice, the guarantor of both individual and collective identity. The aim of Augustine's critique of the Ciceronian city is to generalize grace as a characteristic of human nature in the political realm. For Augustine, grace is the sign of the Christian order; but Spinoza, in the political conclusions of his treatise, emphasizes the notion of individual rights rooted in an autonomy that would have been inconceivable to Augustine. Thus, because of that centrality of human nature (recall the title of chapter 17 of the *Theological-Political Treatise*: "It Is Demonstrated That Nobody Can, or Need, Transfer All His Rights to the Sovereign Power . . ."), the history of the Hebrews can be interpreted as a lesson about what is possible, what is legitimate, and above all, what is *just* in the political. One example, drawn from Roman history, has to do with the question of tyranny. Rome plays a key role here, since it demonstrates the power of freedom defended by Spinoza, a freedom rooted in the "thing of the people": "Now perhaps the Romans will be produced as an example to prove that a people can easily remove a tyrant; but I hold that this example entirely confirms my view. It is true that the Romans found it far easier to remove a tyrant and change the form of their state because the right to appoint the king and his successor was vested in the people itself; and furthermore the people . . . had not yet acquired the habit of obedience to kings."[41]

Everything plays out around the possession of self or, in other words, around the modalities of transfer between the individual and the collectivity, and their political choices. The freedom to think is thus a political freedom: it is derived from the recognition of the right to dispose wholly of oneself, whereas grace is founded on the total offering of self to God in the expectation of divine intervention. For Spinoza, theology cannot tolerate natural enlightenment, since that enlightenment will reveal the absolute role of authority in religious history, in the history of religions. By contrast, philosophy and its freedom, in reinforcing natural enlightenment, can only be founded on individual autonomy, the touchstone of natural religion, its laws and its justice.

In the shift from one city to another, from grace to philosophy, Augustine and Spinoza show the profound connections between the religious and the political. They invite us to think of the individual in terms that are still very familiar to us: autonomy, freedom of choice and expression, will, gift of self and self-control, and finally, the forms of responsibility that define an order and a sociability. In the differences between the two authors, we also find other models for democracy, models not necessarily linked to the Greek legacy. On the contrary, we stand before choices guided by what seems natural both to the theologian and to the philosopher. Hence, for Augustine, "where there is . . . this justice whereby the one supreme God rules the obedient city according to His grace, so that it sacrifices to none but Him . . . in all the citizens of this obedient city, the soul consequently rules the body and reason the vices in the rightful order."[42] Obedience is the visible mark of grace. Even reason is subject to the demands of divine will. It is this submission that Spinoza critiques and rejects in his analysis of superstition and its politics. Furthermore, Spinoza demonstrates that such divine justice, the mirror image and model of monarchical and theocratic powers, is not *natural*. It results from error, from ignorance and, in the end, from a forgetting of self. For, as he says, "I think I have thus demonstrated quite clearly the basis of the democratic state . . . [which] seemed the most natural form of state, approaching most closely to that freedom which nature grants to every man."[43]

Conclusion: "The Infinite Separation"

The difference between Augustine and Spinoza may be summed up by the cleavage between theology and philosophy; or it may lie in the role given to reason in attempts to understand the nature and history of humankind. Although at first sight their paths seem to converge—particularly in how they approach and deal with the legacy of the Old Testament—the two authors are actually in radical opposition. Through a comparison between them, we have been able to grasp the role played by method, the shared foundation of a critical approach, in explaining election and everything that can be associated with it. Their two paths represent tendencies that continue to haunt and incite the modern and contemporary discourse on monotheistic religion, its cultural legacy, and its philosophical interpretation. To illustrate the survival, so to speak, of the Augustine-Spinoza pair, I should like to consider, by way of conclusion, several texts that in some sense attempt to resolve the difficulties produced by the shift—viewed as necessary if not inevitable—from election to grace, or that exploit the turn toward the universal in evaluating the religious. With one exception, these texts are part of what is generally called the "pantheism controversy" in Germany: that is, they are marked by the influence of Spinoza's philosophy.

It is in Kant's work, especially his *Religion within the Limits of Reason Alone*, that we find the clearest and also the most developed expression of the effects of the universal on the representation of the Jewish religion in its relation to Christianity. Inscribed within a problematic that privileges the notion of progress, the ineluctable progress of reason toward humankind's perfection and emancipation, Kant's text posits the cleavage between the local and the universal as a key moment in the religious history of human beings.

Universality is the final goal, the telos, and, above all, the sign of the emergence of the ethical order. Hence, for Kant, within the framework of a revealed faith there can be one and only one religion:

> And now a few words touching this concept of a belief in revelation.
>
> There is only *one* (true) *religion*; but there can be *faiths* of several kinds. We can say further that even in the various churches, severed from one another by reason of the diversity of their modes of belief, one and the same true religion can yet be found.
>
> It is therefore more fitting (as it is more customary in actual practice) to say: This man is of this or that *faith* (Jewish, Mohammedan, Christian, Catholic, Lutheran), than: He is of this or that religion. The second expression ought in justice never to be used in addressing the general public (in catechisms and sermons), for it is too learned and unintelligible for them; indeed, the more modern languages possess no word of equivalent meaning.[1]

Kant seems to reduce the difference between the local and the universal to that between the true church and beliefs, that is, to a difference between a single and unique revealed faith and the variations occasioned by different circumstances and contexts, which, however, all refer to the same starting point, the same origin. The specificity of each belief is acknowledged, but only insofar as it is merely a manifestation of the true religion. Furthermore, Kant applies and generalizes the use of the term "church" to faiths that usually stand outside the realm of Christianity. He therefore associates Judaism and Islam with variations of Christianity. Kant explains that amalgamation in terms of the universal character of the church. For him, "the token of the true church is its *universality*; the sign of this, in turn, is its necessity and its determinability in only one possible way. Historical faith (which is based upon revelation, regarded as an experience) has only particular validity."[2]

The universal is at once general and unique, whereas the local or particular is subject to variations and diversity. Here, slightly modified, is the model set in place by Spinoza when he studies temporal election and its relation to revelation. The difference between Spinoza and Kant in this precise context has to do with the gradual and progressive movement Kant identifies in the evolution of humankind's religious history, and with what he calls "the gradual establishment of the sovereignty of the good principle on earth."[3]

For our purposes, let us simply note two aspects of Kant's analysis, which shed light on the relation between Judaism and Christianity and which characterize the history of Judaism. In the first place, Kant, in keeping with his notion of the universal church as an expression of a divine ethics, distinguishes between Christianity and Judaism. Since there can be only one true church, the history of religion can also only be the history of that church, which contains from its origins the germs of all its later developments: "And first of all it is evident that the Jewish faith stands in no essential connection whatever, *i.e.*, in no unity of concepts, with this ecclesiastical faith whose history we wish to consider, though the Jewish immediately preceded this (the Christian) church and provided the physical occasion for its establishment."[4]

The philosophical examination of religion reduces Judaism to a "physical occasion," a mere moment of transition. In the analytics of universal ethics, everything points to Christianity as the only true religion. In that context, Jewish election or specificity yields to the necessity of ethics, to the inevitability of a progress that does not tolerate local variations and beliefs. That Kantian position gives rise to a description of Judaism that denies it even the name of religion, in the sense Kant understands that word in *Religion within the Limits of Reason Alone*:

> The *Jewish faith* was, in its original form, a collection of mere statutory laws upon which was established a political organization; for whatever moral additions were then or later *appended* to it in no way whatever belong to Judaism as such. Judaism is really not a religion at all but merely a union of a number of people who, since they belonged to a particular stock, formed themselves into a commonwealth under purely political laws, and not into a church; nay, it was *intended* to be merely an earthly state so that, were it possibly to be dismembered through adverse circumstances, there would still remain to it (as part of its very essence) the political faith in its eventual reestablishment (with the advent of the Messiah).[5]

Not a religion but merely a state: here the political prevails over the religious, a radicalization of Spinoza's position and an absolute split between the ethical and the religious on one hand, the political and the local on the other. For Kant, even messianic faith has only political import. That generalization of the political in favor of the ethical leads Kant to formulate a surprising conclusion that solidifies the abandonment or forgetting of Judaism. The history of religion, that is, the history of the universal church, begins and can begin only with Christianity: "We cannot therefore do otherwise than begin general church history, if it is to constitute a system, with the origin of Christianity, which, completely forsaking the Judaism from which it sprang, and grounded upon a wholly new principle, effected a thoroughgoing revolution in doctrines of faith."[6] The history of religion, of universal religion, begins with the history of a first emancipation, that of Christianity, so as to allow the history of the emancipation of reason itself. The universal makes the local and temporal in some sense pointless and superfluous. It reduces them to a relic, to a survival of beliefs. Even that relic, for Kant at any rate, lacks historical foundations. For him, then, the history of Judaism is almost impossible because it was not "subjected to control," that is, to scientific conditions: "Prior to the beginning of Christianity, and even prior to its considerable progress, Judaism had not gained a foothold among the *learned public*, that is, was not yet known to its learned contemporaries among other peoples; its historical recording was therefore not yet subjected to control and so its sacred Book had not, on account of its antiquity, been brought into historical credibility."[7]

For Kant, unlike for Pascal, the antiquity of Judaism is problematic because it lacks witnesses, external witnesses. Inward witnessing, the very same as that valorized by Pascal, is no longer sufficient. We find ourselves in the presence of a scientific imperative for objective confirmation, a need to supersede the local and temporal with something else, something close or similar, we might even say with a comparison.[8] Even Christianity can suffer from the singularity of Jewish history, but it is saved by its universal nature, its dimension as universal ethics, that is, by its desire to share its vision and its beliefs with other peoples, instead of withdrawing into itself and isolating itself in its election. Judaism has an odd fate in Kant's *Religion within the Limits of Reason Alone*: a victim of its origins, a prisoner of its specificity, it is ultimately placed outside history.

Whereas Kant deploys the universal/local dichotomy to describe the relation between Christianity and Judaism, it is primarily Gotthold Lessing, in "The Education of the Human Race" (1780), who will exploit *all* the themes we have already identified between Augustine and Spinoza, from revelation to education to pedagogy. This text is at the heart of the polemics between F. H. Jacobi and Moses Mendelssohn regarding Spinoza's legacy.[9] Let us recall that Lessing chose for his epigraph a line taken from Augustine's *Soliloquies* 2.10: "Haec omnia inde esse in quibusdam vera, unde in quibusdam falsa sunt" (All these things are beholden to the selfsame source, both for their truth and for their falsity). That choice could not be more telling: it is both a continuation of and a deviation from the Augustinian problematics of election and its return as the universalism of grace. Lessing offers us a sort of Spinozan Augustine: while insisting on the unique source of all truth and all things, he renders that uniqueness in Spinozan terms. For Lessing, "What education is to the individual man, revelation is to the whole human race." The revelation given to the Jewish people is a unique choice because God "neither could, nor would, reveal himself any more to *each* individual man, [and therefore] he selected an individual people for his special education; and that the most rude and the most ferocious, in order to begin with it from the very beginning."[10] Lessing explains the shift from the local to the universal as a matter of education. Hence he claims to be resolving "many difficulties" of a theological nature. His depiction of the pedagogical structure implies a determining interpretation, from a theological standpoint, of the individual and his evolution throughout the history of humankind. That depiction brings to mind Augustine's ages of humanity and also Francis Bacon's texts on childhood and youth.

The pedagogical model also allows Lessing to reformulate the modalities of the shift from the Old Testament to the New. The Old Testament has fallen victim to misreadings or misinterpretations that become poor lessons: hence the proliferation of superstitions, obscurantism, uncertainty. Christ, the last and best pedagogue, liberates the Bible from its Jewish childishness and expounds it in its full maturity.[11] The age of truth thus coincides with that of reason, and revelation moves beyond the phase of precursory signs and rough outlines, acceding to historical reality. In that process, election is neither desirable nor necessary: it is a figure from the past and represents only humankind's abandoned childhood. The maturity of humankind, we are not surprised to learn, corresponds to an internalization, an elevation (not to say an election), of adult interiority as the exclusive site of revealed law.

For Lessing, universalism has the appearance of an absolute, flawless equality resting on an equivalence among individuals and among societies, despite the diversity of origins, languages, customs, and histories. But—and this is a completely different story—that universalism is founded on the idea of a single faculty of reason, a reason that takes only a single path, the road of progress and of perfection. Enlightenment reason "passes through"—to borrow Pascal's verb—revelation. Within that context, the status of the chosen people in the Old Testament becomes one of the necessary but provisional stages that prepare for and anticipate the truth and authenticity of revelation. From that viewpoint, in other words, election is the result of a lack, and the choice of the chosen people is no longer the reflection of its privileged status, or of its exchanges with its God, but is rather a divine decision linked to a pragmatics of revelation. Nevertheless, that election gives rise to a special morality, a series of laws limited by the historical conditions of the Jewish people. But then Lessing introduces a second election, as it were, one that supplements the first and whose function is to generalize and universalize the choice of the Jewish people: namely, the education of the Jewish people, which anticipates the education of humankind as a whole. For Lessing, Jewish history is, quite literally, merely a preparatory period, a first stage of humanity, a pre-text. Spinoza's analysis is radicalized: everything is conceived as a function of the ability to recognize a dogma and a truth that are universal. There is an election within the chosen people itself: those who choose to, or have the ability to, move beyond the childishness of their community are, as it were, the chosen among the chosen.

Lessing's pedagogical model, close to the methods of the *Aufklärung*, strives to overcome Spinoza's antitheses (Bible or Truth, theology or philosophy) by adopting the figure of childhood as the sign and symbol of Judaism.[12]

G. W. F. Hegel, by contrast, contests the validity of Lessing's analysis based on pedagogy. In "The Spirit of Christianity and Its Fate," he writes: "The state of Jewish culture cannot be called the state of childhood, nor can its phraseology be called an undeveloped, childlike phraseology."[13]

For Hegel, the Jewish people's election is the history of an "infinite separation," which finds expression in an "expected isolated security" introducing an insurmountable difference between the people of Abraham and the rest of humanity: "Where there is universal enmity, there is nothing left save physical dependence, an animal existence which can be assured only at the expense of all other existence, and which the Jews took as their fief. This exception, this expected isolated security, follows of necessity from the infinite separation."[14]

According to Hegel's analyses, the God of Abraham is a God of the Word, a God who allows for no other; he does not recognize the other or the debt or any remainder. He is the absolutely unique God. Here we return to Augustine and our starting point—between the specificity of Hebrew election and the grace characteristic of Christianity—an explanation of election in terms of the Incarnation. In other words, for Hegel, election, that almost unparalleled "exception," can only be Hebrew; at the same time, however, it is the first condition for Christianity.

As in Augustine's philosophy, election returns to the site of an infinite split, an absolute domination (in Hegelian language), inscribing identity in separation, in the desire for unlimited difference, in the secrets and depths of the incomparable.

NOTES

SELECTED BIBLIOGRAPHY

INDEX

Notes

Preface

1. "They who believe correctly believe, therefore, so that they may call upon him in whom they have believed and may be able to do what they have received in the commandments of the law, because faith obtains what the law commands [*quod lex imperat, fides impetrat*]." Augustine, letter to Hilary (letter 157, 2.8), in *Letters*, part 2, vol. 3 of *The Works of Saint Augustine: A Translation for the Twenty-first Century*, ed. John E. Rotelle, trans. Edmund Hill (Brooklyn, N.Y.: New City Press, 1990–2005), 20. And again: "For this is faith itself, which obtains by prayer what the law commands [*Ipsa est enim fides, quae orando impetrat quod lex imperat*]." Augustine, "On Grace and Free Will" 32, trans. P. Holmes, in *Basic Writings of Saint Augustine*, vol. 1, ed. Whitney J. Oates (New York: Random House, 1948), 759.
2. Augustine, letter to Hilary 2.9, p. 21.
3. Ibid., 3.15, p. 25.
4. Augustine, "On Grace and Free Will" 10, p. 741.

Introduction

1. Henri de Lubac characterizes the originality and specificity of the Christian conception of human nature as follows: "In various forms

and with differences of emphasis, depending on the era and the school, Christian philosophy thus developed the idea of a human nature open to the reception of a supernatural gift. Such a conception was obviously unknown to ancient philosophy." "Le paradoxe ignoré des gentils," repr. in *Le mystère du surnaturel* (Paris: Aubier, 1965), 155.

2. We need to return to Émile Benveniste's analyses in volume 2 of the *Vocabulaire des institutions indo-européennes*, 2 vols. (Paris: Minuit, 1969), on the formation of the "now fundamental pairing of *religion* and *superstition*" and retain above all, at least for this book, the central role of "bearing witness." "[*Religio*] is linked to *relegere*, 'to collect again, to pick up again for a new choice, to return to a prior synthesis in order to recompose it'; *religio*, 'religious scruple,' is thus originally a subjective frame of mind. . . . The interpretation invented by the Christians on the basis of *religare*, 'to bind again,' while historically false, is indicative of the revival of the notion: *religio* becomes 'obligation,' an objective link between the faithful person and his God" (265).

3. Friedrich Nietzsche, *On the Use and Abuse of History*, trans. Adrian Collins, 2nd rev. ed. (Indianapolis: Bobbs-Merrill, 1957), 4 [translation modified—trans.].

1. Augustine, Religion as Rereading

1. Augustine, *On Christian Doctrine* 2.4–5, trans. D. W. Robertson (Indianapolis: Bobbs-Merrill, 1958), 36–37.

2. For the question of translation, see M. Olender, "En quelle langue Dieu a-t-il dit '*Fiat Lux*'?" opening lecture at the twenty-fourth Congress on Literary Translation (Assises de la traduction littéraire), Arles, 2007 (Arles: Atlas/Actes Sud, 2008), 17–31.

3. Augustine, *The Confessions* 1.7, trans. R. S. Pine-Coffin (New York: Penguin, 1988), 28.

4. Ibid., 1.8., p. 29 [translation modified—trans.].

5. Ibid., 10.20.29, pp. 226–227 [translation modified—trans.]. The blessed *(beata)* life is, as it were, a prefiguration of grace: "Human nature, you see, did not receive the power to enjoy the state of bliss independently of God's control, because only God is able to enjoy blessedness and bliss by his own power independently of anyone else's control." "On Genesis—A

Refutation of the Manichees" 2.15.22 in *On Genesis*, part 1, vol. 13 of *The Works of Saint Augustine: A Translation for the Twenty-first Century*, ed. John E. Rotelle, trans. Edmund Hill (Brooklyn, N.Y.: New City Press, 1990–2005), 86.

6. Augustine, *Confessions* 11.3., p. 256 [translation modified]. Clearly, Augustine reconciles the pursuit of happiness and internal truth: "See how I have explored the vast field of my memory in search of you, O Lord! And I have not found you outside it. For I have discovered nothing about you except what I have remembered since the time when I first learned about you. Ever since then I have not forgotten you. For I found my God, who is Truth itself, where I found truth, and ever since I learned the truth I have not forgotten it. So, since the time when I first learned of you, you have always been present in my memory, and it is there that I find you whenever I am reminded of you and find delight in you. This is my holy joy, which in your mercy you have given me, heedful of my poverty" (Augustine, *Confessions* 10.24, p. 230).

7. Ibid., 12.18, p. 296.

8. Augustine, *Eighty-three Different Questions*, question 58, trans. David L. Mosher (Washington, D.C.: The Catholic University of America Press, 1982), 104.

9. Augustine, "On Genesis—A Refutation of the Manichees" 2.1, p. 69.

10. Augustine, *City of God* 22.30, trans. Marcus Dods (New York: Modern Library, 1950), p. 867. "After this period God shall rest as on the seventh day, when they shall give us (who shall be the seventh day) rest in Himself. But there is not now space to treat of these ages; suffice it to say that the seventh shall be Our Sabbath, which shall be brought to a close, not by an evening, but by the Lord's day."

11. Augustine, *Eighty-three Different Questions*, question 53, p. 90.

12. Ibid., question 61, pp. 122–123.

13. Ibid., question 66, p. 141.

14. Augustine, "To Simplician—On Various Questions" 1.2.2., in *Augustine: Earlier Writings*, ed. and trans. John H. S. Burleigh (Philadelphia: Westminster, 1953), 386–387.

15. Augustine, *On Christian Doctrine* 3.8.12, p. 86.

16. Augustine, *Eighty-three Different Questions*, question 65, p. 135.

17. For the details of that reading, see esp. *The Literal Meaning of Genesis*, in *On Genesis*, part 1, vol. 13 of *The Works of Saint Augustine: A Translation for the Twenty-first Century*, ed. John E. Rotelle, trans. Edmund Hill (Brooklyn, N.Y.: New City Press, 1990–2005).

18. Augustine, "To Simplician" 1.1.2, p. 377.

19. This is a recurrent theme in Augustine's analysis in "To Simplician": "Hence it appears that concupiscence was not implanted in him by the law, but was made known [*demonstratam*] to him" (1.2, p. 877).

20. Augustine, *The Literal Meaning of Genesis* 8.18. 37, p. 368. Augustine softens that first response to the question of the divine word in Genesis: "We most certainly have to maintain, however, that God spoke either through his own substance or through some creature subject to him. But then he does not speak through his own substance except for creating all natures, though as regards spiritual and intellectual ones he speaks not only for creating but also for enlightening them, since they are now able to grasp his speeches as it is in his Word, which *was in the beginning with God, and God is what the Word was through whom all things were made* (John 1:1.3). But to those who are not able to grasp this, when God speaks he only does so through a creature, either through a spiritual one alone whether in dreams or in ecstasy in the likeness of bodily things, or also through a bodily one, when some specific appearance is presented to the senses of the body, or some sounds and words are heard" (ibid., 8.27.49, p. 374).

21. Ibid., 11.33.43., pp. 454–455 [translation modified].

22. Augustine, homily 37.4, *Homilies on the Gospel of John 1–40*, part 3, vol. 12 of *The Works of Saint Augustine: A Translation for the Twenty-first Century*, ed. John E. Rotelle, trans. Edmund Hill (Brooklyn: New City Press, 1990–2005), 567. And: "So then, the Word came first. And what was there before the Word of God? Nothing whatsoever. In fact, if there had been anything before, it would not be said, *In the beginning was the Word*, but 'In the beginning was made the Word'" (ibid., 37.8, p. 572).

23. Augustine, *The Trinity* 2.7.32, part 1, vol. 5 of *The Works of Saint Augustine: A Translation for the Twenty-first Century*, ed. John E. Rotelle, trans. Edmund Hill (Brooklyn, N.Y.: New City Press, 1990–2005), 120 [translation modified—trans.].

24. Ibid., 3.4.22, pp. 140–141.

25. Augustine, "To Simplician" 2.2, p. 386.

26. Ibid., 1.6, p. 390 [words in brackets do not appear in the published English translation—trans.]

27. That economic dimension of grace is prefigured in Augustine's text by a discussion of the verb "render" *(reddet)*: "Do you think, perhaps, that because he said 'shall render' he meant that it was his due [*jam fit ex debito*]? But when 'he ascended on high and took captivity captive, he' did not render but '*gave* gifts to men [*dedit dona hominibus*]' [Eph 4:8]. How could the apostle speak presumptuously as of a debt being paid back to him, unless he had first received grace which was not due to him, being justified by which, he fought the good fight?" (Ibid., 388).

28. Augustine, sermon 212, in *Sermons*, part 3, vol. 6 of *The Works of Saint Augustine: A Translation for the Twenty-first Century*, ed. John E. Rotelle, trans. Edmund Hill (Brooklyn, N.Y.: New City Press, 1990–2005), 136 [translation modified].

29. Augustine, *The Retractations* 2.69, trans. Mary Inez Bogan, vol. 60 of *The Fathers of the Church* (Washington, D.C.: The Catholic University of America Press, 1968), 210 [translation modified: the translation has "vision" for "dream"—trans.]. In the introduction to the French translation, the editors note the unique status of this book: "Saint Augustine's *Retractations* occupies a place apart, not only in the history of ancient Christian literature but in that of literature generally, and it cannot be placed in any of the categories, numerous though they may be, that the makers of treatises have imagined." Introduction to Saint Augustine, *Les révisions*, trans. Gustave Bardy (Paris: Desclée de Brouwer, 1950), 11.

30. Augustine, *Retractations* 1.21, p. 93 [the words "precepts and promises" appear in brackets in the published English translation of Augustine—trans.].

31. See the chapter titled "L'âme de saint Augustin d'après les *Révisions*," in Augustine, *Les révisions*, 217–248.

32. Augustine, *The City of God* 10.3.2, pp. 306–307 [translation modified—trans.].

33. Saint Augustine, "Answer to Adimantus, a Disciple of Mani" 2.2. in *The Manichean Debate*, part 1, vol. 19 of *The Works of Saint Augustine: A Translation for the Twenty-first Century*, ed. John E. Rotelle, trans. Edmund Hill (Brooklyn, N.Y.: New City Press, 1990–2005), 177.

34. Ibid., 9.1, pp. 186–187.

35. To give just a sample of the Manichaean view of the Old and New Testaments according to Augustine: "They say that the law given by means of Moses, the servant of God, did not come from the true God but from the prince of darkness" (letter 236, in *Letters*, part 2, vol. 4 of *The Works of Saint Augustine: A Translation for the Twenty-first Century*, ed. John E. Rotelle, trans. Edmund Hill [Brooklyn, N.Y.: New City Press, 1990–2005], 134); "This disputation is to be considered as directed against the Manichaeans, who do not accept the Scripture of the Old Testament, where an account of original sin is given, and who maintain, with detestable arrogance, that what is read about it in the Apostolic writings was interpolated by corruptors of the Scriptures as though it had not been said by the Apostles themselves" (*Retractations* 1.8.6, p. 39); and finally: "They claimed that the books of the New Testament had been tampered with by unnamed persons who wished to impose the Jewish law upon the Christian faith" (*Confessions* 5.11.21, pp. 105–106).

36. Augustine, "The Grace of Christ and Original Sin" 24–25.29, in *Answer to the Pelagians*, part 1, vol. 23 of *The Works of Saint Augustine: A Translation for the Twenty-first Century*, ed. John E. Rotelle, trans. Edmund Hill (Brooklyn, N.Y.: New City Press, 1990–2005), 448.

37. "We are God's coinage, coins that have gone astray from the treasury" (homily 40.9, in *Homilies on the Gospel of Saint John 1–40*, 603. For other coins, Augustinian in particular, see M. Olender, "Mot, monnaie et démocratie: Lieux communs de l'intime," in *Origines du langage: Une encyclopédie poétique*, ed. Olivier Pot, *Le genre humain* 45–46 (2007): 523–549.

38. Augustine, *Sermons*, sermon 211, p. 128.

39. "As your good life [for which eternal life is given] is nothing else than God's grace, while the eternal life, which is the recompense of a good life, . . . is grace for grace [*gratia est pro gratia*], as if a wage for justice; in order that it may be true, because it is true, that God 'shall reward every man according to his works'" (Augustine, "On Grace and Free Will" 20, trans. P. Holmes, in *Basic Writings of Saint Augustine*, vol. 1, ed. Whitney J. Oates [New York: Random House, 1948], p. 749) [translation modified; words in brackets do not appear in the English translation—trans.].

40. Augustine, *Sermons*, sermon 212, p. 136. "Symbolum autem nuncupatur a similitudine quadam translato vocabulo quia symbolum inter se

faciunt mercatores quo eorum societas pacto fidei teneatur. Et vestra societas est mercium spiritualium ut similes sitis negotiatoribus bonam margaritam quaerentibus. Hac erit caritas quae diffundetur in cordibus vestris per spiritum sanctum qui dabitur vobis."

41. For a recent overview of the question, see M. Olender, "Ce que le politique doit au poétique," in *La conscience de soi de la poésie. Colloques de la Fondation Hugot du Collège de France (1993–2004)*, ed. Yves Bonnefoy, *Le genre humain* 47 (2008): 135–160, esp. 143–146.

42. Émile Benveniste, *Vocabulaire des institutions indo-européennes*, 2 vols. (Paris: Minuit, 1969), esp. the article "Créance et croyance," 1:171–179.

43. Augustine, *Sermons*, sermon 212, p. 138.

44. Ambrose of Milan, *Des sacrements. Des mystères*, trans. Bernard Botte (Paris: Cerf, 1994), 57–59 [my translation from the French—trans.]. Recall as well the episode in which Victorinus recites his symbol, as recounted in Augustine's *Confessions* 8.2.5, pp. 150–161.

45. Augustine, "On Grace and Free Will" 24, p. 752 [translation modified: the translation has "righteousness" and "righteous" for "justice" and "just" respectively—trans.].

46. Letter to Hilary (letter 157, 3.15), in *Letters*, part 2, vol. 3 of *The Works of Saint Augustine: A Translation for the Twenty-first Century*, ed. John E. Rotelle, trans. Edmund Hill (Brooklyn, N.Y.: New City Press, 1990–2005), 25 [translation modified—trans.].

47. Augustine, *Expositions on Psalms* 102.11, part 3, vol. 19 of *The Works of Saint Augustine: A Translation for the Twenty-first Century*, ed. John E. Rotelle, trans. Edmund Hill (Brooklyn, N.Y.: New City Press, 1990–2005), 92. "God's law, you see, was written by the finger of God, but because of their hard hearts it was written on stone. Now the Lord was finally writing in earth, because he was looking for it to bear fruit." Augustine, *Homilies on the Gospel of John*, homily 33.5, p. 528.

48. The Vulgate translates the passage from Jeremiah as follows: "Sed hoc erit pactum quod feriam cum domo Israhel post dies illos dicit Dominus dabo legem meam in visceribus eorum et in corde eorum scribam eam et ero eis in Deum et ipsi erunt mihi in populum."

49. Pierre Courcelle, *Les Confessions de saint Augustin dans la tradition littéraire* (Paris: Études augustiniennes, 1963), 109.

50. Athanasius of Alexandria, *The Life of Antony* 55, in *The Life of Antony and the Letter to Marcellinus*, trans. Robert C. Gregg (New York: Paulist Press, 1980), 72–73.

51. Augustine, *Confessions* 2.3, p. 45.

52. "The Trinity appeared in the clearest possible way: the Father in the voice, the Son in the man, the Spirit in the dove" (Augustine, *Homilies on the Gospel of John*, homily 6.5, p. 125).

53. Augustine, *Homilies on the Gospel of John*, homily 23.8, p. 413. "You have already, I gather, grasped the way in which *perhaps* is to be taken; so let no weigher of words or scrutinizer of syllables, as if he were well versed in speaking Latin, find fault with the word which was uttered by the Word of God, and thus remain, by finding fault with the Word of God, not eloquent but dumb. Who after all, speaks in the way which the Word—*which was in the beginning with God* (Jn 1:1)—speaks? . . . Within you, my good man, when a word is in your heart, it is something other than a sound; but for the word which is in you to reach me, it seeks a sound as a vehicle. So it takes a sound, climbs somehow or other onto this vehicle, goes through the air, reaches me, and does not leave you. But for the sound to reach me, it did leave you, and did not remain with me. So then, the word which was in your heart did not go away when the sound went away, did it? You said what you were thinking, and for what was hidden in you to reach me, you put syllables together, in a sound; the sound of the syllables carried your thought to my ears, your thought climbed down through my ears into my heart, the sound which acted as intermediary flew away. But that word, which took on sound, was with you before you uttered it; because you did utter it, it is now with me and has not left you. Pay attention to that, whoever you are, you scrutinizer of sounds, you belittle the Word of God, you who do not understand the word of a human being" (homily 37.4, in *Homilies on the Gospel of John 1–40*, 567).

54. Augustine, *The Trinity* 3.11.26, p. 144 [translation modified—trans.]. And again: "I must also acknowledge, incidentally, that by writing I have myself learned much that I did not know" (ibid., 3.1.1, p. 127).

55. Augustine, *The City of God* 19.21.1, p. 699 [translation modified—trans.]. For Cicero's text, see Maurice Testard, *Saint Augustin et Cicéron*, 2 vols. (Paris: Études augustiniennes, 1958), esp. 1:207.

56. For the commentary on the Ciceronian definition of the republic, see Augustine, *The City of God* 19.21.1, p. 699.

57. Ibid., 19.23.6, pp. 705–706 [translation modified: the translation has "righteousness" for "justice"—trans.].

58. An Augustinian definition of superstition: "Among superstitious things is [*Superstitionium est*] whatever has been instituted by men concerning the making and worshiping of idols, or concerning the worshiping of any creature or any part of any creature as though it were God. Of the same type are things instituted concerning consultations and pacts involving prognostications with demons who have been placated or contracted with. These are the endeavors of the magic arts, which the poets are accustomed to mention rather than to teach" (Augustine, *On Christian Doctrine* 2.20.30, p. 55). Augustine also devotes an important passage in the *City of God* (4.30.1, p. 137) to Cicero's attempts to distinguish superstition from religion.

2. Hobbes, or Nature as Reason

1. Thomas Hobbes, *On the Citizen*, ed. and trans. Richard Tuck and Michael Silverthorne (New York: Cambridge University Press, 1996), 7. In my remarks on Hobbes, I have limited myself to this text because *Leviathan* only reaffirms and continues the analysis and conclusions of *On the Citizen*.

2. Ibid., preface, 12.

3. Ibid., 172 [italics in all the quotations from *On the Citizen* are in the published English translation—trans.].

4. Ibid. Hobbes speaks of the "triple word of God" (171).

5. Ibid., 188.

6. Ibid.

7. Ibid., 189–190 [translation modified: the translation has "supernaturally" for "by supernatural grace"—trans.].

8. Ibid., 190 [translation modified].

9. Ibid., 196.

10. Ibid., 200.

11. Ibid., 208–209.

12. Ibid., 174 [translation modified: the translation has "weakness" in place of "imbecility"—trans.]. Hobbes adds the following remark to explain man's imbecility: *"If anyone thinks this harsh, I ask him to reflect quietly, if there were two who were omnipotent, which one would be obligated to obey the other. It will be admitted, I believe, that neither is obligated to the other. If this is true, my point is also true, that men are subject to God primarily because they are not omnipotent. For when our Saviour warned Paul (who was at that time an enemy of the Church) not to kick against the pricks, He seems to have required obedience from him on the ground that he did not have strength to resist"* (175).

13. Ibid., preface, 11.

3. Spinoza and the "Relics of Man's Ancient Bondage"

1. Benedictus de Spinoza, *Theological-Political Treatise*, trans. Samuel Shirley (Indianapolis: Hackett, 1998), 1–2. For a French translation of the passage, see Benedictus de Spinoza, *Oeuvres III. Traité théologico-politique*, ed. Fokke Akkerman, trans. Jacqueline Lagrée and Pierre-François Moreau (Paris: PUF, 1999), 59, where the last sentence reads, "So long as fear can make men rave."

2. Spinoza, *Theological-Political Treatise*, 3–4 [translation modified—trans.].

3. Ibid., 3.

4. Benedictus de Spinoza, *Ethics*, trans. Andrew Boyle, rev. G. H. R. Parkinson (London: Dent, 1989), 32–33.

5. Spinoza, *Theological-Political Treatise*, 37.

6. Ibid.

7. "Therefore whatever human nature can effect solely by its own power to preserve its own being can rightly be called God's internal help, and whatever falls to a man's advantage from the power of eternal causes can rightly be called God's external help" (ibid., 37).

8. Ibid., 39.
9. Ibid., 40.
10. Ibid., 39.
11. Ibid., 40.
12. Ibid., 45.

13. Ibid., 47.
14. Ibid., 47–48.
15. Judah Halevi, *The Kuzari: An Argument for the Faith of Israel*, trans. Hartwig Hirschfeld (New York: Schocken, 1964).
16. [The title of Judah's book is sometimes rendered as "Kuzari: In Defense of the Despised Religion"—trans.]
17. Ibid., 1.26–29, p. 47 [translation modified].
18. Ibid., 1.115, p. 79 [translation modified].
19. Ibid, 2.12, pp. 88–89 [brackets appear in the published English translation of Judah—trans.].
20. Ibid., 1:95, pp. 65–66 [translation modified—trans.].
21. Ibid., 2.68, p. 124 [translation modified—trans.].
22. Ibid., 4.17, p. 224.
23. Spinoza, *Theological-Political Treatise*, 54.
24. Ibid., 29.
25. Ibid., 57.
26. Ibid., 12.
27. Ibid., 14.
28. Ibid.
29. Ibid., 55, 61.
30. Ibid., 166.
31. Ibid., 169.
32. Ibid., 167 and 168.
33. Blaise Pascal, *Pensées*, trans. A. J. Krailsheimer (New York: Penguin, 1966), 204/592, pp. 95–96. For the *Pensées*, I give both the fragment number from the Lafuma edition of Pascal's *Oeuvres complètes*, ed. Louis Lafuma (Paris: Seuil, 1963) and that of the Brunschvicg edition: *Oeuvres*, ed. Léon Brunschvicq (Paris: Hachette, 1904–1914). Hence, "204/592" signifies: Lafuma fragment 204, Brunschvicg fragment 592. [The Penguin edition follows the numbering of Lafuma—trans.]
34. Ibid., 436/628, pp. 165–166.
35. Ibid., 573/646, p. 224 [translation modified].
36. Ibid., 454/619, p. 176.
37. Ibid., 822/593, p. 276.
38. Ibid., 328/732, p. 129.
39. Ibid., 289/608, pp. 120–121.

40. Spinoza, *Theological-Political Treatise*, 179.
41. Ibid., 218.
42. Augustine, *The City of God* 19.23.6, trans. Marcus Dods (New York: Modern Library, 1950), 705–706 [translation modified].
43. Spinoza, *Theological-Political Treatise*, 185.

Conclusion

1. Immanuel Kant, *Religion within the Limits of Reason Alone*, trans. Theodore M. Green and Hoyt H. Hudson (New York: Harper, 1960), 98.
2. Ibid., 105.
3. Part of the title of section 2 of Kant's *Religion within the Limits of Religion Alone*, 115.
4. Ibid., 116.
5. Ibid.
6. Ibid., 118.
7. Ibid., 154.
8. Ibid., 154–155.
9. For an overview of the pantheism controversy, see Pierre-Henri Tavoillot, *Le crépuscule des Lumières. Les documents de la querelle du panthéisme, 1780–1789* (Paris: Cerf, 1995). This volume also contains a French translation of Lessing's "Education of the Human Race."
10. Gotthold Ephraim Lessing, "The Education of the Human Race," in *Lessing's Theological Writings: Selections in Translation*, trans. Henry Chadwick (Stanford, Calif.: Stanford University Press, 1956), 82 and 83.
11. "A better instructor must come and tear the exhausted primer from the child's hands—Christ came!" Ibid., 91.
12. Lessing also valorizes the inward turn as a distinctive mark of Christianity: "To preach an inward purity of heart in reference to another life, was reserved for [Christ] alone" (Ibid., 91).
13. G. W. F. Hegel, "The Spirit of Christianity and Its Fate," in *On Christianity: Early Theological Writings by Friedrich Hegel*, trans. T. M. Knox with Richard Kroner (New York: Harper and Brothers, 1961), 256.
14. Ibid., 191.

Selected Bibliography

Augustine

English-language Editions

Augustine: Earlier Writings, edited and translated by John H. S. Burleigh. Philadelphia: Westminster, 1953.
Basic Writings of Saint Augustine. Vol. 1. Edited by Whitney J. Oates. New York: Random House, 1948.
The City of God, translated by Marcus Dods. New York: Modern Library, 1950.
The Confessions, translated by R. S. Pine-Coffin. New York: Penguin, 1988.
Eighty-three Different Questions, translated by David L. Mosher. Washington, D.C.: The Catholic University of America Press, 1982.
On Christian Doctrine, translated by D. W. Robertson. Indianapolis: Bobbs-Merrill, 1958.
The Retractations, translated by Mary Inez Bogan. Vol. 60 of *The Fathers of the Church*. Washington, D.C.: The Catholic University of America Press, 1968.
The Works of Saint Augustine: A Translation for the Twenty-first Century, edited by John E. Rotelle, translated by Edmund Hill. Brooklyn, N.Y.: New City Press, 1990–2005.

French Editions

Les oeuvres de saint Augustine. Paris: Desclée de Brouwer, 1941–2008.
Les révisions. Paris: Desclée de Brouwer, 1950
Oeuvres I. Paris: Gallimard, 1998.
Oeuvres II. La Cité de Dieu. Paris: Gallimard, 2000.
Oeuvres III. Paris: Gallimard, 2002.
Sermons pour la Pâques. Paris: Cerf, 1966.

Latin Edition

Patrologiae cursus completus. Series latina. Ed. Jean-Paul Migne. Paris, 1844–1864.

Critical Works

Arendt, Hannah. Love and Saint Augustine, edited by Joanna Vecchiarelli Scott and Judith Chelius Stark, translated by E. B. Ashton with revisions by the author. Chicago: University of Chicago Press, 1996.
Brown, Peter Robert Lamont. Augustine of Hippo: A Biography. New ed. Berkeley: University of California Press, 2000.
Courcelle, Pierre. Les Confessions de saint Augustin dans la tradition littéraire. Paris: Études augustiniennes, 1963.
———. Recherches sur les Confessions de saint Augustin. Paris: Boccard, 1968.
Gilson, Étienne. Philosophie et Incarnation selon Augustin. Montreal: Institut d'études médiévales, 1947.
———. Introduction à l'étude de saint Augustin. Paris: Vrin, 1982.
Lubac, Henri de. Le mystère du surnatural. Paris: Aubier, 1965.
Madec, Goulven. Le Dieu d'Augustin. Paris: Cerf, 1998.
Marrou, Henri-Irénée. L'ambivalence du temps de l'histoire chez saint Augustin. Montreal: Institut d'études médiévales, 1950.
———. Saint Augustin et la fin de la culture antique. Paris: Boccard, 1983 [1958].
Olender, Maurice. "En quelle langue Dieu a-t-il dit 'Fiat Lux'?" Opening lecture at the twenty-fourth Congress on Literary Translation (Assises

de la traduction littéraire), Arles, 2007. Arles: Atlas/Actes Sud, 2008, 17–31.

———. "Mot, monnaie et démocratie: Lieux communs de l'intime." In *Origines du langage. Une encyclopédie poétique*, ed. Olivier Pot. *Le genre humain* 45–46 (2007): 523–549.

———. "Ce que le politique doit au poétique." In *La conscience de soi de la poésie. Colloques de la Fondation Hugot du Collège de France (1993– 2004)*, ed. Yves Bonnefoy. *Le genre humain* 47 (2008): 135–160.

Stock, Brian. *Augustine the Reader: Meditation, Self-Knowledge, and the Ethics of Interpretation*. Cambridge, Mass.: Belknap Press of Harvard University Press, 1996.

Testard, Maurice. *Saint Augustin et Cicéron*. 2 vols. Paris: Études augustiniennes, 1958.

Spinoza

English-Language Editions

Ethics, translated by Andrew Boyle, revised by G. H. R. Parkinson. London: Dent, 1989.

Theological-Political Treatise, translated by Samuel Shirley. Indianapolis: Hackett, 1998.

French Editions

Oeuvres complètes. Paris: Gallimard, 1954.

Traité théologico-politique, translated by Charles Appuhn. Paris: Garnier-Flammarion, 1965.

Bilingual Latin/French Editions

Éthique, translated by Bernard Pautrat. Paris: Seuil, 1999 [1988].

Oeuvres III. Traité théologico-politique, edited by Fokke Akkerman, translated by Jacqueline Lagrée and Pierre-François Moreau. Paris: PUF, 1999.

Critical Works

Albiac, Gabriel. *La sinagoga vacía: Un estudio de las fuentes marranas del espinosismo*. Madrid: Hiperión, 1987. (French edition: *La Synagogue vide: Les sources marranes du spinozisme*, translated by Marie-Lucie Copete and Jean-Frédéric Schaub. Paris: PUF, 1994.)

Atlan, Henri. *Les étincelles de hasard*. 2 vols. Paris: Seuil, 1999 and 2003.

Brykman, Geneviève. *La Judéité de Spinoza*. Paris: Vrin, 1982.

Deleuze, Gilles. *Spinoza et le problème de l'expression*. Paris: Minuit, 1968.

———. *Spinoza. Philosophie pratique*. Paris: Minuit, 1981.

Lazzeri, Christian. *Droit, pouvoir et liberté: Spinoza critique de Hobbes*. Paris: PUF, 1998.

Matheron, Alexandre. *Individu et communauté chez Spinoza*. Paris: Minuit, 1969.

———. *Le Christ et le salut des ignorants chez Spinoza*. Paris: Aubier-Montagine, 1971.

———. *Anthropologie et politique au XVIIe siècle: Études sur Spinoza*. Paris: Vrin, 1986.

Moreau, Pierre-François. *Spinoza. L'expérience et l'éternité. Recherches sur la constitution du système spinoziste*. Paris: PUF, 1994.

Révah, Israël S. *Spinoza et le docteur Juan de Prado*. Paris: Mouton, 1959.

———. *Des Marranes à Spinoza*, edited by Henry Méchoulan, Pierre-François Moreau, and Carsten-Lorenz Wilke. Paris: Vrin, 1995.

Zac, Sylvain. *Spinoza et l'interprétation de l'Écriture*. Paris: PUF, 1965.

Other Books Cited

Ambrose of Milan. *Des sacrements. Des mystères*, translated by Bernard Botte. Paris: Cerf, 1994.

Athanasius of Alexandria. *The Life of Antony and the Letter to Marcellinus*, translated by Robert C. Gregg. New York: Paulist Press, 1980. (French edition: *Vie d'Antoine*, translated into French by Gerhardus Johannes Marinus Bartelink. Paris: Cerf, 1994.)

Benveniste, Émile. *Vocabulaire des institutions indo-européennes*. 2 vols. Paris: Minuit, 1969.

Selected Bibliography

Hegel, G. W. F. "The Spirit of Christianity and Its Fate." In *On Christianity: Early Theological Writings by Friedrich Hegel*, translated by T. M. Knox with Richard Kroner. New York: Harper and Brothers, 1961. (French editions: *L'esprit du Christianisme et son destin*, translated by Jacques Martin. Paris: Vrin, 1988; and *L'esprit du Christianisme et son destin, précédé de l'esprit du judaïsme*, translated by Olivier Depré. Paris: Vrin, 2003.)

Hobbes, Thomas. *On the Citizen*, edited and translated by Richard Tuck and Michael Silverthorne. New York: Cambridge University Press, 1996. (French edition: *Le citoyen*. Paris: Garnier-Flammarion, 1982.)

Hobeika, Georges. *Lessing: De la révélation à âge adulte de la raison*. Paris: Cerf, 1997.

Judah Halevi. *The Kuzari: An Argument for the Faith of Israel*, translated by Hartwig Hirschfeld. New York: Schocken, 1964. (French edition: *Le Kuzari*. Lagrasse: Verdier, 2001 [1994].)

Kant, Immanuel. *Religion within the Limits of Reason Alone*, translated by Theodore M. Green and Hoyt H. Hudson. New York: Harper, 1960. (French edition: *La religion dans les limites de la simple raison*, translated by Monique Naat. Paris: Vrin, 2000.)

Lessing, Gotthold Ephraim. "The Education of the Human Race." In *Lessing's Theological Writings: Selections in Translation*, translated by Henry Chadwick. Stanford, Calif.: Stanford University Press, 1956.

Nietzsche, Friedrich. *On the Use and Abuse of History*, translated by Adrian Collins. 2nd rev. ed. Indianapolis: Bobbs-Merrill, 1957. (French edition: *Considérations inactuelles*, translated into French by Pierre Rusch. 2 vols. Paris: Gallimard, 1990.)

Pascal, Blaise. *Oeuvres*, edited by Léon Brunschvicq. Paris: Hachette, 1904–1914.

———. *Oeuvres complètes*, edited by Louis Lafuma. Paris: Seuil, 1963.

———. *Pensées*, translated by A. J. Krailsheimer. New York: Penguin, 1966.

Tavoillot, Pierre-Henri. *Le crépuscule des Lumières*. Paris: Cerf, 1995. Includes a French translation of Lessing's "The Education of the Human Race."

Index

Abraham, 21, 29, 54–56, 71–72, 92
Acts of the Apostles, 25–26, 29, 34
Adam, 17, 35, 42, 54, 72–75
allegory, 5, 18–20
Ambrose of Milan, 40
"Answer to Adimantus," 29
Antichrist, 77
antiquity of Judaism, 80, 89
Antony, Saint, 45–46
Athanasius, 45
Aufklärung, 92
Augustine, Saint: on cities, 52–53; comparisons of, 1–7, 16, 25, 57–61, 64, 75, 77–92; on religion, 9–51
autonomy: and election, 26; and freedom, 4, 7; and grace, 26, 82–84

bearing witness, 2, 26, 28, 44, 79, 81–82, 89
Benveniste, Émile, 38, 96n2
Bible, 2, 59. *See also* New Testament; Old Testament
bondage, 37–38, 58–84

charity, 38, 50–51, 78
childhood, 16, 57, 90–92
Christian city, 34, 52–53. *See also* cities

Christian doctrine, 9
Christian liberty, 19–20
Christian visibility, 20, 24–25
Christianity: contesting, 77; and Judaism, 7–8, 33, 43–46, 77, 80, 87–92; and rereading, 9–51
church: defining, 57; and faiths, 86–87; going astray, 77; history of, 87; as institution, 57; as mystical body, 71; as symbol, 7; and synagogue, 30; universal, 87–88; visibility of, 80
Cicero, 49–51, 82–83
circumcision: command about, 55; and election, 63–67; rite of, 69–70
cities, 34, 48–53, 82–84
City of God, 4, 17, 29, 48, 97n10
coinage, 37–38, 100n37
comparisons, 1–8, 16, 25, 57–64, 75–92.
  See also Christianity; Judaism
confession, 35, 46–47
Confessions, 11–12, 14, 16, 30, 32, 45
conversion, 3, 11, 15, 19–20, 31–32, 37, 42–47, 69–70
Courcelle, Pierre, 45
creation of humankind, 12, 16–18, 34.
  See also humankind

Creation symbols, 17, 97n10. *See also* symbols
De Republica, 49
"despised religion," 68, 69
diversity, 10–13, 63–64, 70, 86–87
divine justice, 52–53, 84
divine language, 16, 21–23, 46–47, 72–73, 98n20, 98n22, 102n53
divine speech, 53–55, 57, 65, 73–76
divine will: access to, 20; demands of, 84; and election, 73; expression of, 11, 19; and faith, 55; and language, 16; and memory, 22; repository of, 43; truth of, 12, 15–16

Ecclesia, 18, 71
education, 89–92
"Education of the Human Race, The," 89–90
election: and autonomy, 26; and childhood, 16; and circumcision, 63–67; contesting, 77–78; and divine will, 73; and error, 74–76; and grace, 17–20, 23–28, 33–35, 41–44, 58–59, 90, 92; interpretation of, 68–73; and language, 16; and Law, 9, 24, 27, 31–32, 43, 67, 76–77; as legacy, 69, 70; and merit, 27; notion of, 64–65, 71–73, 77–78; proof of, 81–82; question of, 1–2; understanding, 1–4; visibility of, 23, 78–83
errors, 73–78, 84
Ethics, 59, 61
Eve, 54, 72, 75

faith: and church, 86–87; and diversity, 86–87; and divine will, 55; and Law, 26; and obedience, 77–78; and piety, 64, 78
fear, 60–61, 75
freedom, 4, 7, 77, 82–84

genealogy, 3, 32–33
Genesis, 16–17, 19, 32, 73
gestures, 12–13, 34, 67

God: language of, 16, 21–23, 72–73; nature of, 59, 61–64, 77; purpose of, 27; visibility of, 20, 22. *See also* divine speech; divine will
Gospel of John, 44–47
grace: accepting, 4; and autonomy, 26, 82–84; economy of, 10, 25, 28, 36, 78, 99n27; and election, 17–20, 23–28, 33–35, 41–44, 58–59, 90, 92; and humanity, 16–19, 35, 50; and Law, 6–7, 14, 18, 27, 42, 47–48; and obedience, 84; question of, 2; and rereading, 32; theme of, 50

Halevi, Judah, 68–71, 73
happiness, desiring, 13, 97n6
heart, 40–48, 58–60
Hegel, G. W. F., 92
historical progress, 18, 20
history: of humankind, 16–18, 20, 28, 75, 85–87, 91; of languages, 11; translating, 10
Hobbes, Thomas, 52–58
Homilies on the Gospel of John, 44
human communication, 13, 54
human heart, 43–48
human law, 41–42, 52–57, 74–77
human nature, 4, 95–96n1, 96–97n5
human speech, 13, 54
humanity and grace, 16–19, 35, 50
humankind: creation of, 12, 16–18, 34; and grace, 16–19, 35, 50; history of, 16–18, 20, 28, 75, 85–87, 91; pick of, 68–73; representation of, 57
humility, 50–51

ignorance, 50, 57, 60–63, 75, 84
Iliad, 80
imbecility, 53–57, 104n12
Incarnation: economy of, 14, 23–25, 47; and Law, 18–19; necessity of, 20, 22, 37; truth of, 5; visibility of, 28, 33, 35, 37–38
individual choice, 35, 50, 84, 90
interiority: adult, 91; and comparisons, 8; and concealment, 26, 28; language

Index

of, 16, 45, 47; and memory, 13; nature of, 4, 43; privilege of, 39; and rediscovery, 37; return to, 15, 41; visibility of, 43, 47

Jacobi, F. H., 90
Jeremiah, 44
Jewish "nationalism," 6
Jewish superstition, 4. *See also* superstition
John, 44–48
Josiah, King, 56
Judaism: antiquity of, 80, 89; and Christianity, 7–8, 33, 43–46, 77, 80, 87–92; critique of, 25; transcendence of, 14
justice, divine, 52–53, 84

Kant, Immanuel, 86–90
Kuzari, 68–73, 75

languages: diversity of, 10–13; divine, 16, 21–23, 46–47, 72–73, 98n20, 98n22, 102n53; and divine will, 16; and election, 16; history of, 11; of scripture, 9–10, 15–18, 64–68, 72–78
law: human, 41–42, 52–57, 74–77; natural, 42, 52–57, 75; political, 87, 88; universal, 76–77
Law: and election, 9, 24, 27, 31–32, 43, 67, 76–77; and faith, 26; and fear, 60–61; function of, 20; and grace, 6–7, 14, 18, 27, 42, 47–48; hiding behind, 33–34; and Incarnation, 18–19; and prophecy, 66; reading of, 31–32; and reason, 42–43; and superstition, 4; and symbol, 41
Lessing, Gotthold, 89–92
Literal Meaning of Genesis, The, 19, 32
Logos, 46–47
Lubac, Henri de, 95–96n1

Manichaeans, 6, 33–34, 100n35
mankind, pick of, 68–73. *See also* humankind
mediation, 73–78

memory: and divine will, 22; and happiness, 13, 97n6; and interiority, 13; and language, 12–13; and symbols, 39
Mendelssohn, Moses, 90
merit, 27
Moses, 14, 21, 30, 34–36, 42–45, 55–56, 64, 72, 75–76
Mount Sinai, 29–30
"mutual transactions," 28

nationalism, 6
natural law, 42, 52–57, 75
nature: of God, 59, 61–64, 77; law of, 52–57; as reason, 52–57
New Testament: gift of, 41; and Old Testament, 3–6, 24, 29–30, 34, 78; transition to, 3–6, 40, 90–91
Nietzsche, Friedrich, 8, 77

obedience: and authority, 5, 54, 59, 73–74, 83; and faith, 77–78; and grace, 84
Old Testament: attitude toward, 33; and New Testament, 3–6, 24, 29–30, 34, 78; prophecies of, 3, 5, 15, 20, 59, 82; revelations of, 6, 59; study of, 48–49; transition from, 3–6, 40, 90–91; translation of, 14–15
"On Genesis—A Refutation of the Manichees," 32
On the Citizen, 53

paganism, 4, 48–51, 59
"pantheism controversy," 85–86, 106n9
Pascal, Blaise, 72–73, 78–83, 89, 91
Pascalian exception, 78–83
Paul, Saint, 17, 43, 46, 66
pedagogy, 83, 90, 92
Pelagian crisis, 6
Pensées, 73, 80
Pentateuch, 64
philosophy, 4, 77, 82–84
piety and faith, 64, 78
political choices, 3–4. *See also* individual choice
political dimension, 3, 39, 41, 61, 82–84

political law, 87, 88
political realities, 48–51
prejudice, 5, 24–25, 61–63, 75
prophecies: and bearing witness, 81–82; and Law, 66; of Old Testament, 3, 5, 15, 20, 59, 82

reading: and Christianity, 9, 19–20; as political act, 3; and religion, 9–51; and visibility, 18–19; ways of, 2–8, 15–20, 28–34, 37; and writing, 45–46
religion: conception of, 32–33; as rereading, 9–51
Religion within the Limits of Reason Alone, 86, 89
rereading: religion as, 9–51; ways of, 2–8, 15–20, 28–29, 34, 37
Retractations, 28–29, 31, 99n29

Sara, 30
Scipio, 49
scripture: interpretation of, 5; language of, 9–10, 15–18, 64–68, 72–78; and symbols, 33–41
self-reading, 18, 37
Sermon on the Mount, 29–30
Sibylline, 80
signs, interpreting, 7, 19. *See also* symbols
Simplician, 20
sociability, 52, 57, 84
social order, 13, 52, 57, 84
Soliloquies, 90
speech: divine, 53–55, 57, 65, 73–76; human, 13, 54; learning, 11–12
Spinoza, Benedictus de: and bondage, 58–84; comparisons of, 1–7, 16, 25, 85–92; and political realities, 48–51
"Spirit of Christianity and Its Fate, The," 92
Stephen, 34

"supernatural grace," 55
superstition, 4–5, 51, 59–65, 75, 84, 90, 96n2, 103n58
symbols: of Creation, 17, 97n10; interpreting, 7, 19; and Law, 41; and memory, 39; and scripture, 33–41; writing, 29, 38–41, 45–46
synagogue, 80

theological pedagogy, 83, 90, 92
theological-political argument, 61
theological-political dimensions, 3, 82
Theological-Political Treatise, 2, 25, 43, 51, 58–59, 63, 68, 74, 77, 83
theology and philosophy, 3, 82, 85
"To Simplician—Questions on Various Subjects," 9
tolerance, 57, 78
Treatise on the Symbol, 40
Trinity, 22–24, 47–48
Trinity, The, 32, 48
Trismegistus, 80

Ummah, 71
universal language, 12–13
universal law, 76–77
universalism, 4–7, 86–92
universality, 4–7, 28, 34–35, 44–48, 64, 75, 86–92

viscera, 40, 43–45, 58, 59
visibility: economy of, 25; of election, 23, 78–83; of God, 20, 22; of Incarnation, 28, 33, 35, 37–38; of interiority, 43, 47; and reading, 18–20
Vita Antonii, 45–46

witness, bearing, 2, 26, 28, 44, 79, 81–82, 89
writing and symbols, 29, 38–41, 45–46

Harvard University Press is a member of Green Press Initiative (greenpressinitiative.org), a nonprofit organization working to help publishers and printers increase their use of recycled paper and decrease their use of fiber derived from endangered forests. This book was printed on recycled paper containing 30% post-consumer waste and processed chlorine free.